TRADER JOE'S

FAVORITE

Sunset

RECIPES

By the Editors of Sunset Books and Sunset Magazine

Sunset Publishing Corporation • *Menlo Park, California*

OUR READERS' FAVORITES

At *Sunset*, we've been collecting wonderful recipes for over 60 years. This special edition presents the cream of the crop: more than 125 reader-selected favorites, old and new. In *Trader Joe's Favorite Sunset Recipes*, you'll find not only rich, traditional choices like fondue and oatmeal chocolate chip cookies, but also some of the leaner, fresher dishes made popular in recent years. And each one is tried and true. • Throughout this book, we've included numerous special features; some focus on perennially popular dishes—pancakes, sandwich spreads, and rice dishes—while others offer advice on culinary techniques. Pages 48–49, for example, lists a number of suggestions for cooking fish. In each chapter, you'll also notice text boxes highlighting some of the special ingredients available at Trader Joe's. • For their help in selecting recipes, we thank Bernadette Hart, Reader Service Coordinator, *Sunset* Magazine, and Rita Burgelman, *Sunset* Hospitality Manager. • We thank Rebecca LaBrum for editing the original manuscript and Carrie Sanders for editorial assistance. • For each of our recipes, we provide a nutritional analysis (see page 5) prepared by Hill Nutrition Associates, Inc., of Florida.

SUNSET BOOKS
President and Publisher
Susan J. Maruyama
Director, Finance & Business
Gary Loebner
Director, Manufacturing & Sales Service
Lorinda Reichert
Western Regional Sales Director
Richard A. Smeby
Eastern Regional Sales Director
Richard M. Miller
Editorial Director
Kenneth Winchester
Coordinating Editor
Cornelia Fogle
Developmental Editor
Lynne Gilberg
Assistant Editor
Kevin Freeland
Research & Text
Lisa Chaney
Contributing Editors
Annabel Post and Tori Ritchie
Design
Susan Sempere
Illustrations
Dick Cole

SUNSET PUBLISHING CORPORATION
Chairman
Robert L. Miller
President/Chief Executive Officer
Robin Wolaner
Chief Financial Officer
James E. Mitchell
Circulation Director
Robert I. Gursha
Editor, Sunset Magazine
William R. Marken
Senior Editor (Food and Entertaining)
Sunset Magazine
Jerry Anne Di Vecchio

Cover: Design by Susan Bryant and Image Network. Photography by Darrow M. Watt

Second Printing October 1995
Copyright © Sunset Publishing
Corporation, Menlo Park, CA 94025
First edition. All rights reserved, including
the right of reproduction in whole or in
part in any form.

ISBN 0-376-00134-8
Library of Congress Catalog Card Number
94-067824
Printed in the United States.

For more information on Trader Joe's
Favorite Sunset Recipes or any other
Sunset book, call (800) 634-3095.
For special sales, bulk orders, and
premium sales information, call
Sunset Custom Publishing Services at
(415) 324-5577.

 printed on recycled paper

CONTENTS

·

Special Features

Our All-Time Favorites

From creamy cheese dishes to satisfying, seafood stews, favorite recipes rank high among life's pleasures. These are the never-fail supper standbys for busy work weeks and the impressive introductions to company dinners or holiday feasts. • For over 60 years, Sunset has reported on trends in Western cooking. We've printed thousands of recipes—some created here, others taken from around the world. We have provided a forum both for new ingredients and techniques and for the time-honored specialties that remain popular year after year.

Time-tested Recipes

Recently we asked our readers to select their all-time *Sunset* favorites, old and new—any recipe published from 1929 to the present was eligible for nomination. Replies came in by the hundreds, including votes for over 1,000 recipes. Of these, more than 125 appear in this volume, along with features, tips on cooking methods, and specialty ingredients. *Sunset* printed similar cook books in 1949, 1969, and 1982—and in *Trader Joe's Favorite Sunset Recipes*, we present yet another comprehensive recipe collection, covering everything from simple family fare to elegant choices for entertaining.

For each recipe, we offer a complete nutritional analysis. If your favorites are higher in fat and calories than you'd like, you may want to use the nutritional information to help keep your diet on track.

We've included some of the culinary lore about a few dishes. Certain recipes are flagged as "Western Classics." These are long-time favorites created in the West, often showcasing our native ingredients. Others are flagged because they showcase *Trader Joe's* ingredients.

Reader Participation

From our earliest issues, we've encouraged reader contributions and suggestions. Our monthly recipe exchanges, "Kitchen Cabinet" and "Chefs of the West," help us keep up with trends in food and entertaining, letting us know what Westerners are cooking at home. Close attention to our readers' interests plays a big part in the signature *Sunset* style—a style that treasures tradition, but also explores all the ingredients and attitudes popular with today's home cook.

Comfort Food

Many of *Sunset*'s best-loved dishes are undeniably the rich "comfort foods" of earlier years. In the following pages, you'll find dozens of such favorites, among them Hasty Hots, Swiss Fondue,

Pecan-topped Sweet Potatoes and Big Oatmeal Chocolate Chip Cookies. Neither Western in origin nor "modern" in appeal, these classics are prized for both their wonderful flavor and their nostalgic, old-time charm.

Dining al Fresco

We like to cook and eat outdoors. Dining al fresco suits the informal Western style—and because our climate is so mild, patio barbecues and picnic meals are pleasant in almost any season. We've become experts in grilling just about everything: meats, fish, poultry, even fresh produce.

Picnics are featured in our pages nearly every year. In 1946, *Sunset* came up with the "tailgate picnic," an idea that has since caught on all over the country. Sandwiches are among our most popular picnic choices, of course, and on pages 21–23, you'll find both hot and cold varieties.

Fresh Ingredients

Western cooks are blessed with a wealth of fresh ingredients, from wonderful fruits and vegetables to top-quality poultry and shellfish. And we've always made a point of introducing our readers to locally available foods. In 1929, we ran features on both avocados and artichokes; more recently, we've highlighted market

newcomers like pomelos, Asian pears, tropical fruits, and organic lettuces, as well as an increasing selection of locally produced cheeses and Pacific seafood. Dishes made with everything from mangoes and lemon grass to Northwest salmon have joined our list of cherished favorites.

For those who might not have ready access to well-stocked markets, we're careful to suggest more widely available alternatives to fresh foods, many of them available at Trader Joe's.

Western Style Evolves

The international influence on Western cooking distinguishes many *Sunset* recipes. Early ethnic specialties included Mexican and Italian fare such as guacamole, enchiladas, and lasagne. In recent years, we've expanded our regional cuisine to embrace the foods and culinary

techniques of Latin America, Southeast Asia, the Orient, and the Pacific islands. Guided by *Sunset* articles, our readers have learned to use all kinds of new ingredients and methods, bringing the flavors of various foreign cuisines to their everyday meals.

About Our Nutritional Data

•

For our recipes, we provide a nutritional analysis stating calorie count; percentage of calories from fat; grams of protein, carbohydrates, total fat, and saturated fat; and milligrams of cholesterol and sodium. Generally, the analysis applies to a single serving, based on the number of servings given for each recipe and the amount of each ingredient. If a range is given for the number of servings and/or the amount of an ingredient, the analysis is based on an average of the figures given.

The nutritional analysis does not include optional ingredients or those for which no specific amount is stated. If an ingredient is listed with a substitution, the information was calculated using the first choice.

APPETIZERS

In the last 50 years, few aspects of our culture have changed more dramatically than the way we entertain. Early Sunset menus featured elegant hors d'oeuvres that were passed to guests before dressy sit-down dinners or luncheons. But entertaining has since become far more relaxed. Today's parties are rarely as formal as yesterday's, nor are they as time-consuming to arrange. In Sunset's pages, the "walk-around" party came into vogue, boosting the popularity of dips, tortas, and other simple "eaten-out-of-hand" specialties. Our recipes also mirrored the West's ethnic diversity, including ideas from Mexico, France, and Southeast Asia. • In this chapter, you'll find a bit of everything— from Super Nachos and Soy-Chili Chicken Wings to Dried Tomato Torta and Zucchini Madeleines. Hot or cold, simple or more elaborate, all have become often-requested favorites.

Melted Brie in a Crust

Readers like this recipe. It looks impressive and tastes wonderful, and it's a cinch to prepare. You just fit a round of Brie into a hollowed-out loaf of French bread, then bake. Delicious!

- **1 round or oval loaf (about 1 lb.) day-old French bread**
- **⅓ cup olive oil; or ⅓ cup butter or margarine, melted**
- **2 cloves garlic, minced or pressed**
- **1 to 1½ pounds Brie, Camembert, or St. André cheese**

With a serrated knife, cut straight down through top of bread to leave a shell about ½ inch thick on all sides; do not cut through bottom crust. Slide your fingers down into cuts and pull center of loaf free in a single piece, leaving a ½-inch-thick base in shell. Around rim of shell, make cuts 1½ inches deep and 1½ inches apart. Cut bread from center of loaf into ½-inch-thick slices; set aside.

In a small bowl, combine oil and garlic. Brush inside of shell with about 3 tablespoons of the oil; brush bread slices with remaining oil. Place cheese in bread shell, trimming to fit. You may leave rind on cheese or trim it off.

Place filled shell and bread slices in a single layer in a 10- by 15-inch rimmed baking pan. Bake in a 350° oven until bread slices are toasted (about 10 minutes). Remove slices to a rack to cool. Continue to bake filled shell until cut edges of bread are golden and cheese is melted (about 10 more minutes).

Place filled shell on a board; surround with toasted bread slices to dip into melted cheese. When all bread slices have been eaten, snap off crisp pieces from edge of shell for dippers. Makes about 40 servings.

Per serving: 96 calories (57 percent from fat), 4 g protein, 6 g carbohydrates, 6 g total fat (0.3 g saturated fat), 15 mg cholesterol, 155 mg sodium

---

Western Classic

Creamy Crab Dip

Fill artichokes or avocado halves with this flavorful spread.

- **1 large package (8 oz.) cream cheese, at room temperature**
- **2 tablespoons *each* dry white wine and lemon juice**
- **1 clove garlic, minced or pressed**
- **1 teaspoon Dijon mustard**
- **½ teaspoon Worcestershire**
- **¼ cup thinly sliced green onions**
- **½ pound crabmeat or surimi**
  Salt and pepper
  Assorted crackers

In a large bowl, beat cream cheese, wine, lemon juice, garlic, mustard, and Worcestershire with an electric mixer until smoothly blended. Stir in onions and crab. Season to taste with salt and pepper. If made ahead, cover and refrigerate until next day. Serve with crackers. Makes about 2 cups.

Per tablespoon: 33 calories (72 percent from fat), 2 g protein, 0.4 g carbohydrates, 3 g total fat (2 g saturated fat), 15 mg cholesterol, 47 mg sodium

---

Fresh Mushroom Pâté

To vary the taste and texture of this traditional recipe, use different varieties of fresh mushrooms.

- **¼ cup butter or margarine**
- **⅓ pound regular or shiitake mushrooms (or a combination), coarsely chopped**
- **⅓ cup finely chopped onion**
- **1 tablespoon dry sherry or chicken broth**
- **1 small package (3 oz.) cream cheese, at room temperature**
- **¼ cup minced parsley**
  Toasted baguette slices, crackers, or crisp raw vegetables

Melt butter in a wide frying pan over medium heat. Add mushrooms and onion; cook, stirring often, until mush-

---

rooms are browned (about 15 minutes). Stir in sherry.

In a small bowl, beat cream cheese and parsley until blended. Stir in mushroom mixture. If made ahead, cover and refrigerate for up to 3 days; bring to room temperature before serving. Serve with bread. Makes about 1 cup.

Per tablespoon: 49 calories (86 percent from fat), 0.7 g protein, 1 g carbohydrates, 5 g total fat (3 g saturated fat), 14 mg cholesterol, 46 mg sodium

---

Shrimp Cheese Stack

Tiny shrimp and spicy chili sauce add variety to seasoned cream cheese. Spread the combination on crisp crackers.

- **2 large packages (8 oz. *each*) cream cheese, at room temperature**
- **2 tablespoons Worcestershire**
- **¼ teaspoon grated lemon peel**
- **1 tablespoon lemon juice**
- **½ cup thinly sliced green onions**
- **⅛ teaspoon liquid hot pepper seasoning**
- **1 bottle (about 12 oz.) tomato-based chili sauce**
- **1 tablespoon prepared horse-radish**
- **¾ pound small cooked shrimp**
  Assorted crackers

In a large bowl, beat cream cheese, Worcestershire, lemon peel, lemon juice, onions, and hot pepper seasoning with an electric mixer until smoothly blended. Spoon mixture into a wide, shallow serving dish and smooth top. (At this point, you may cover and refrigerate until next day.)

Just before serving, stir together chili sauce and horseradish in a small bowl; spread over cheese layer. Top with shrimp. Serve with crackers. Makes 12 to 16 servings.

Per serving: 166 calories (62 percent from fat), 8 g protein, 8 g carbohydrates, 12 g total fat (7 g saturated fat), 83 mg cholesterol, 502 mg sodium

Layered Cheese Torta with Pesto

Layers of aromatic pesto and delicate, buttery cheese have made this simple, yet dramatic appetizer a *Sunset* favorite since it first appeared in our pages in 1983. Like the traditional cheese tortas of Italy, it should be served with crisp toasts.

Easy Pesto (recipe follows)
2 **large packages (8 oz. *each*) cream cheese or Neufchâtel cheese, at room temperature**
1½ **cups (¾ lb.) unsalted butter (do not use margarine), at room temperature**
    Basil sprigs
    Toasted baguette slices or crisp raw vegetables

Prepare Easy Pesto and set aside. In a large bowl, beat cream cheese and butter with an electric mixer until smoothly blended.

You will need a 5- to 6-cup straight-sided plain mold such as a tall brioche or charlotte pan (or use a loaf pan). Line mold with a double thickness of cheesecloth (large enough to hang over sides of mold) which has been moistened with water and wrung dry.

With a rubber spatula, spread a sixth of the cheese mixture in mold. Cover with a fifth of the pesto, spreading it evenly to sides of mold. Repeat to use remaining cheese and pesto, finishing with cheese.

Fold ends of cloth over mold; press down lightly with your hands to compact. Refrigerate until torta feels firm when pressed (1 to 1½ hours); unfold cloth from top, invert torta onto a serving dish, and gently pull off cloth. (If torta is chilled in its mold for over 1½ hours, cloth will act as a wick and cause pesto color to bleed onto cheese.) If made ahead, cover and refrigerate for up to 5 days.

To serve, garnish torta with basil sprigs. Serve with bread. Makes 16 servings.

Easy Pesto. In a blender or food processor, combine 2½ cups lightly packed **fresh basil leaves,** 1 cup (about 4 oz.) grated **Parmesan or Romano cheese,** and ⅓ cup **olive oil.** Whirl to form a paste. Stir in ¼ cup **pine nuts;** season to taste with **salt** and **pepper.**

Per serving: 342 calories (89 percent from fat), 6 g protein, 3 g carbohydrates, 35 g total fat (19 g saturated fat), 83 mg cholesterol, 219 mg sodium

Marinated Cheese

Cheeses marinated in oil and herbs make a simple, satisfying appetizer—and when packed in attractive glass containers, they're lovely gifts. To vary the flavor, you might include a different selection of fresh seasonal herbs or use a flavored olive oil.

8 **ounces feta cheese or unripened goat cheese (such as Montrachet); or 3 slightly soft whole breakfast cheeses (about 3 oz. *each*)**
    About 5 fresh or dry marjoram, rosemary, oregano, or thyme sprigs (*each* about 3 inches long); or 2 tablespoons *total* of the dry herbs, crushed
3 **cloves garlic, peeled**
5 **or 6 Niçoise olives, salt-cured olives, or Spanish-style green olives**
    About ½ cup olive oil
    Toasted baguette slices or assorted crackers

If using feta cheese, cut into large chunks; if using goat cheese, cut into 1½-inch-thick slices. If using breakfast cheeses, leave whole.

Fit cheese compactly into a small (about 1½-cup) jar or crock. Add herbs, garlic, and olives. Fill jar with oil to cover cheese; cover jar and refrigerate for at least 5 days or up to 6 weeks (oil congeals, but liquefies at room temperature).

To serve, bring to room temperature. Serve with bread. Makes 6 to 8 servings.

Per serving: 229 calories (88 pervent from fat), 5g protein, 2 g carbohydrates, 23 g total fat (7g saturated fat), 29 mg cholesterol, 388 mg sodium

Olive-filled Cheese Balls

These hot tidbits have been reader favorites for over 30 years. To make each bite-size treat, just wrap an olive in a layer of flaky Cheddar pastry.

1 **cup (about 4 oz.) shredded sharp Cheddar cheese**
2 **tablespoons butter or margarine, at room temperature**
½ **cup all-purpose flour**
    Dash of ground red pepper (cayenne)
25 **medium-size pitted ripe or pimento-stuffed green olives, drained well**

In a small bowl, beat cheese and butter until well blended. Stir in flour and red pepper. Wrap 1 to 2 teaspoons of dough around each olive, covering completely. Place 1 inch apart on a baking sheet. Bake in a 400° oven until pastry is crisp but not browned (12 to 15 minutes). Makes 25 appetizers.

Per appetizer: 40 calories (64 percent from fat), 1 g protein, 2 g carbohydrates, 3 g total fat (2 g saturated fat), 7 mg cholesterol, 71 mg sodium

Dips are classic party starters. The recipes we offer here may not be new, but you can easily give them a fresh look by updating the accompaniments. Crisp leaves of baby romaine serve as scoops for heartier dips; toasted pita triangles, bagel chips, and crunchy breadsticks are excellent choices too. Out-of-the-ordinary vegetables such as yellow cherry tomatoes, baby bok choy, jicama, or wild mushrooms can give a simple herb dip an exotic air.

Green Goddess Dip

1 clove garlic, minced or pressed
¼ cup *each* coarsely chopped parsley, sliced green onions, and coarsely chopped watercress
1 teaspoon *each* dry tarragon and anchovy paste
2 teaspoons lemon juice
½ cup *each* mayonnaise and sour cream
   Onion salt

In a blender or food processor, combine garlic, parsley, onions, watercress, tarragon, anchovy paste, and lemon juice; whirl until smoothly puréed. Stir in mayonnaise and sour cream until well blended. Season to taste with onion salt. Makes about 1½ cups.

Per tablespoon: 45 calories (93 percent from fat), 0.3 g protein, 0.5 g carbohydrates, 5 g total fat (1 g saturated fat), 5 mg cholesterol, 37 mg sodium

Aïoli

7 or 8 large cloves garlic, minced or pressed
1 egg
   Yolk of 1 hard-cooked egg
1 tablespoon lemon juice
1 cup olive oil
   Salt

In a blender or food processor, combine garlic, egg, hard-cooked egg yolk, and lemon juice; whirl until blended. With motor running, add oil in a thin, steady stream, whirling until blended. Season to taste with salt. Serve at room temperature. Makes about 1½ cups.

Per tablespoon: 87 calories (96 percent from fat), 0.4 g protein, 0.4 g carbohydrates, 9 g total fat (1 g saturated fat), 18 mg cholesterol, 3 mg sodium

Hot Artichoke Cheese Dip

1 can (about 8½ oz.) water-packed artichoke hearts, drained and chopped
1 jar (about 6 oz.) marinated artichoke hearts, drained and chopped
1 small can (about 4 oz.) diced green chiles
⅓ cup mayonnaise
1½ to 2 cups (6 to 8 oz.) shredded Cheddar cheese

Spread canned and marinated artichokes in a well-greased shallow 2-quart baking pan (or 7- by 11-inch baking pan). Scatter chiles on top, then spread mayonnaise over all. Sprinkle evenly with cheese; then cover pan with foil and bake in a 350° oven until bubbly and heated through (about 15 minutes). Serve hot. Makes about 2½ cups.

Per tablespoon: 39 calories (76 percent from fat), 1 g protein, 0.9 g carbohydrates, 3 g total fat (1 g saturated fat), 6 mg cholesterol, 82 mg sodium

Red Pepper Dip

3 tablespoons olive oil
3 large onions, thinly sliced
2 jars (about 7 oz. *each*) roasted red peppers, drained
2 teaspoons fresh thyme leaves or 1 teaspoon dry thyme
2 tablespoons tomato paste
½ cup *each* grated Parmesan cheese and ricotta cheese
   Thyme sprigs (optional)

Heat oil in a wide frying pan over medium-low heat. Add onions and cook until very soft and golden (about 30 minutes); stir occasionally at first, then more often as onions begin to turn golden. Onions should not show signs of browning during the first 15 minutes; if they do, reduce heat.

Add peppers, thyme leaves, and tomato paste to onions; cook, stirring often, for 5 more minutes. Let mixture cool slightly.

In a blender or food processor, whirl pepper mixture, Parmesan cheese, and ricotta cheese until puréed. Transfer to a serving bowl. If made ahead, cover and refrigerate until next day. Serve cold or at room temperature; garnish with thyme sprigs, if desired. Makes about 4 cups.

Per tablespoon: 17 calories (58 percent from fat), 0.6 g protein, 1 g carbohydrates, 1 g total fat (0.3 g saturated fat), 1 mg cholesterol, 18 mg sodium

Dried Tomato Torta

We like dried tomatoes for their versatility and tart, pungent flavor. They're sold both loose (like dried fruit) and packed in oil; this torta, created in 1988, uses the oil-packed variety. Serve the rich spread with toasted sliced French bread or pita triangles.

1 **large package (8 oz.) cream cheese or Neufchâtel cheese, at room temperature**
1 **cup (½ lb.) unsalted butter (do not use margarine), at room temperature**
1 **cup (about 4 oz.) grated Parmesan cheese**
½ **cup dried tomatoes packed in oil, drained (reserve oil)**
   About 2 cups lightly packed fresh basil leaves
   Toasted baguette slices or pita bread wedges

In a large bowl, beat cream cheese, butter, and Parmesan cheese with an electric mixer until smoothly blended; set aside.

Cut 4 of the tomatoes into thin strips; cover and refrigerate. In a blender or food processor, whirl remaining tomatoes, 2 tablespoons of the reserved oil from tomatoes, and ½ cup of the cheese mixture until puréed. Add purée to remaining cheese mixture and beat until creamy. Cover and refrigerate until firm enough to shape (about 20 minutes); then mound on a platter. If made ahead, cover and refrigerate for up to 3 days.

To serve, arrange basil leaves and reserved tomato strips around torta. Spread torta on bread; for extra flavor, top cheese with a basil leaf and a tomato strip. Makes 12 to 16 servings.

Per serving: 232 calories (84 percent from fat), 5 g protein, 4 g carbohydrates, 22 g total fat (13 g saturated fat), 60 mg cholesterol, 205 mg sodium

Zucchini Madeleines

For a savory twist on the traditional shell-shaped cakes of France, try these unusual, cheese-laced bites.

1 **pound zucchini, shredded**
2 **teaspoons salt**
6 **tablespoons olive oil**
1 **medium-size onion, chopped**
5 **eggs**
2 **tablespoons milk**
1½ **cups (about 6 oz.) grated Parmesan cheese**
1 **clove garlic, minced or pressed**
2 **tablespoons chopped fresh basil or 1 teaspoon dry basil**
¼ **teaspoon pepper**
1 **cup all-purpose flour**
1 **tablespoon baking powder**

In a colander, mix zucchini with salt. Let stand until zucchini is limp and liquid has drained from it (about 30 minutes). Rinse and drain zucchini well, squeezing out as much water as possible.

While zucchini is draining, heat 2 tablespoons of the oil in a wide frying pan over medium-high heat. Add onion and cook, stirring often, until soft (about 4 minutes). Remove pan from heat.

In a large bowl, beat eggs, milk, remaining ¼ cup oil, cheese, garlic, basil, and pepper with a wire whisk until blended. Add zucchini and onion and mix well. Add flour and baking powder; stir just until evenly moistened.

Spoon batter into greased, floured madeleine pans (1½- or 2-tablespoon size) or tiny (about 1½-inch) muffin pans, filling to rims. Bake in a 400° oven until puffed and lightly browned (about 15 minutes for 1½-tablespoon madeleines, about 18 minutes for 2-tablespoon madeleines, about 20 minutes for muffins). Let cool for 5 minutes; invert pans to remove madeleines. Serve hot or cooled.

If made ahead, let cool completely, then wrap airtight; refrigerate until next day or freeze for longer storage (thaw before reheating). To reheat, place madeleines in a single layer on baking sheets and heat, uncovered, in a 350° oven until warm (about 5 minutes). Makes about 3 dozen appetizers.

Per appetizer: 70 calories (60 percent from fat), 3 g protein, 4 g carbohydrates, 5 g total fat (1 g saturated fat), 33 mg cholesterol, 258 mg sodium

TRADER JOSÉ'S
Super Nachos

Ground beef, spicy sausage, beans, and chiles "beef up" the traditional nacho base of melted cheese and tortilla chips.

- ½ **pound** *each* **lean ground beef and chorizo, casings removed; or use 1 pound lean ground beef and omit chorizo**
- 1 **large onion, chopped**
  Salt
  Liquid hot pepper seasoning
- 1 **or 2 cans (about 1 lb.** *each***) refried beans**
- 1 **small can (about 4 oz.) diced green chiles**
- 2 **to 3 cups (8 to 12 oz.) shredded jack or mild Cheddar cheese**
- ¾ **cup purchased green or red taco sauce**
  Crisp-fried Tortilla Pieces (recipe follows) or about 8 cups purchased tortilla chips
  Garnishes (suggestions follow)

Crumble beef and sausage into a wide frying pan. Add onion and cook over medium-high heat, stirring often, until meat is lightly browned. Discard fat; season meat mixture to taste with salt and hot pepper seasoning.

Spread beans in a large, shallow baking pan. Top evenly with meat mixture. Sprinkle with chiles, cover evenly with cheese, and drizzle with taco sauce. (At this point, you may cover and refrigerate until next day.)

Prepare Crisp-fried Tortilla Pieces.

Bake bean-meat mixture, uncovered, in a 400° oven until heated through (20 to 25 minutes). Remove pan from oven. Immediately add garnishes: mound avocado dip and sour cream in center, then add green onions, olives, pickled pepper, and cilantro sprigs as desired. Tuck Crisp-fried Tortilla Pieces around edges of bean mixture and serve at once. If desired, keep pan hot on a warming tray. Makes 12 to 16 servings.

Crisp-fried Tortilla Pieces. Stack 12 **corn tortillas;** cut stack into 6 equal wedges. In a deep 2- to 3-quart pan, heat about ½ inch of **salad oil** over medium-high heat to 350° to 375°F on a deep-frying thermometer. Add one stack of wedges; stir to separate. Cook until crisp (1 to 1½ minutes); lift from oil with a slotted spoon and drain on paper towels. Repeat to cook remaining wedges. If desired, sprinkle lightly with **salt.** If made ahead, let cool; store airtight until next day.

Garnishes. Have ready 1 can (about 8 oz.) **frozen avocado dip,** thawed (or 1 medium-size ripe avocado, pitted, peeled, coarsely mashed, and mixed with 1 tablespoon lemon juice); 1 cup **sour cream;** about ¼ cup thinly sliced **green onions;** about 1 cup **pitted ripe olives;** 1 **mild red pickled pepper;** and **cilantro or parsley sprigs.**

Per serving: 282 calories (51 percent from fat), 14 g protein, 20 g carbohydrates, 16 g total fat (2 g saturated fat), 37 mg cholesterol, 544 mg sodium

TRADER MING'S
Soy-Chili
Chicken Wings

Sunset's food editors discovered these spicy-hot chicken wings during a trip through China in 1987. After we published this recipe, they quickly became a favorite.

- 2 **pounds chicken wing drumettes**
- 2 **tablespoons salad oil**
- ¼ **cup soy sauce**
- 2 **tablespoons rice wine or dry sherry**
- 2 **tablespoons sugar**
- 1 **teaspoon chili oil or 2 small dried hot red chiles**
- 4 **quarter-size slices fresh ginger**
- 2 **cloves garlic, peeled**
- 2 **green onions**
- 1 **cup water**

Rinse chicken and pat dry. Heat salad oil in a wide frying pan over high heat. Add chicken, a portion at a time (do not crowd pan); cook, turning as needed, until browned on all sides. Return all chicken to pan, then add soy sauce, wine, sugar, chili oil, ginger, garlic, whole onions, and water. Bring to a boil. Then reduce heat, cover, and simmer until meat near bone is no longer pink; cut to test (about 20 minutes). Uncover and boil, turning chicken often, until sauce is thick enough to coat wings (10 minutes). If made ahead, let cool; cover and refrigerate until next day. Serve warm or at room temperature; to reheat, place chicken in a single layer on baking sheets and heat in a 350° oven until warm. Makes 8 servings.

Per serving: 179 calories (54 percent from fat), 15 g protein, 5 g carbohydrates, 11 g total fat (2 g saturated fat), 62 mg cholesterol, 579 mg sodium

Cocktail Walnuts

Crisp walnuts (or pecans or almonds) seasoned with soy and ginger are tasty alongside your favorite beverage.

- 2 **tablespoons butter or margarine, melted**
- 2 **teaspoons soy sauce**
- ½ **teaspoon** *each* **ground ginger and salt**
- ¼ **teaspoon garlic powder**
- 2 **cups (about ½ lb.) walnut halves or pieces**

In a 9- by 13-inch baking pan, combine butter, soy sauce, ginger, salt, and garlic powder; mix well. Add walnuts and stir to coat; then spread out in a single layer. Bake in a 250° oven until crisp (about 45 minutes), stirring occasionally. Let cool, then store airtight for up to 1 month. Makes 2 cups.

Per ¼ cup: 209 calories (83 percent from fat), 4 g protein, 5 g carbohydrates, 20 g total fat (3 g saturated fat), 8 mg cholesterol, 255 mg sodium

The choice of a beverage, like that of a party hat, is subject to whim and fancy. And just as much as the rest of the menu, the drinks you serve help set the mood of the meal. These classic recipes, some of them more than a few decades old, incorporate ingredients and ideas from all over the world, from Scandinavia to the tropics.

Chilled Citrus Sangría

- 2 **bottles (about 750 ml. *each*) dry red wine**
- 4 **cups fresh orange juice**
- 1 **cup *each* fresh lime juice and fresh lemon juice**
- ½ **cup sugar, or to taste**
- 4 **cups sparkling water or club soda, chilled**
  Orange slices
  Crushed ice or ice cubes

In a large bowl, stir together wine, orange juice, lime juice, lemon juice, and sugar. Cover and refrigerate until cold.

Just before serving, stir in sparkling water and garnish with orange slices. Ladle into ice-filled glasses. Makes about 4 quarts.

Per cup: 127 calories (2 percent from fat), 0.7 g protein, 17 g carbohydrates, 0.1 g total fat (0 g saturated fat), 0 mg cholesterol, 18 mg sodium

Lemon Grass Lemonade

- **Lemon Grass Syrup (recipe follows)**
- 5 **cups water**
- 6 **tablespoons lemon juice**
  Crushed ice or ice cubes

Prepare Lemon Grass Syrup; pour into a 2-quart pitcher and stir in water and lemon juice. Cover and refrigerate until next day. To serve, pour into ice-filled glasses. Makes about 6 cups.

Lemon Grass Syrup. Cut off leafy tops and peel tough outer layers from 3 stalks **fresh lemon grass.** Trim off and discard discolored or dry parts of root ends; cut stalks into 2-inch lengths and crush lightly with a mallet (or thinly slice stalks crosswise).

In a 1- to 1½-quart pan, combine lemon grass and 1 cup *each* **sugar** and **water.** Bring to a boil over high heat; reduce heat and simmer, uncovered, until syrup is reduced to 1 cup (about 30 minutes). Let cool. If made ahead, cover and refrigerate for up to 2 weeks. Discard lemon grass before using syrup.

Per cup: 132 calories (0.3 percent from fat), 0.1 g protein, 34 g carbohydrates, 0 g total fat (0 g saturated fat), 0 mg cholesterol, 4 mg sodium

Ginger Punch

- 1 **small pineapple (3 to 3½ lbs.), peeled, halved, cored, and cut into 1-inch chunks; or 4 cups pineapple juice**
- 4 **cups water**
- ¼ **pound fresh ginger, scrubbed and cut into 1-inch chunks**
- ½ **cup lemon juice**
- ¾ **cup sugar, or to taste**
  Crushed ice or ice cubes

Whirl pineapple chunks, a portion at a time, in a blender or food processor with 2 cups of the water until puréed. Pour purée through a fine strainer into a large bowl, squeezing and pressing pulp to remove juice; discard pulp. (If using pineapple juice, simply mix it with 2 cups water in a large bowl.)

Place ginger in blender or food processor with remaining 2 cups water; whirl until puréed. Then pour purée through strainer into pineapple juice, squeezing liquid from pulp; discard pulp. Stir in lemon juice and sugar. Pour into a pitcher, cover, and refrigerate un-

til cold. To serve, stir well and pour into ice-filled glasses. Makes about 2 quarts.

Per cup: 154 calories (1 percent from fat), 0.7 g protein, 39 g carbohydrates, 0.2 g total fat (0 g saturated fat), 0 mg cholesterol, 6 mg sodium

Hot Cranberry Glögg

- 4 **cups cranberry-apple juice cocktail**
- 2 **cups dry red wine**
- ¾ **cup *each* sugar and water**
- 1 **cinnamon stick (3 to 4 inches long)**
- 3 **whole cardamom pods, lightly crushed**
- 4 **whole cloves**
  Thin orange slice
- ½ **cup *each* raisins and whole blanched almonds**

In a large glass or stainless steel bowl, combine juice cocktail, wine, sugar, water, cinnamon stick, cardamom, and cloves. (At this point, you may cover and refrigerate for up to 2 days.)

To serve, pour punch into a 3- to 4-quart pan; warm over medium heat just until heated through. Float orange slice on top. Keep warm over a candle or on a warming tray, if desired. Ladle into cups or mugs, adding raisins and almonds to individual servings. Makes about 2 quarts.

Per cup: 278 calories (17 percent from fat), 2 g protein, 50 g carbohydrates, 5 g total fat (0.5 g saturated fat), 0 mg cholesterol, 8 mg sodium

Nonalcoholic Cranberry Glögg

Follow directions for **Hot Cranberry Glögg,** but omit wine, sugar, and water. Increase cranberry-apple juice cocktail to 6 cups. Makes about 7 cups.

Per cup: 233 calories (20 percent from fat), 3 g protein, 46 g carbohydrates, 5 g total fat (0.5 g saturated fat), 0 mg cholesterol, 7 mg sodium

Happy Hour Mushrooms

A reader from Sacramento sent this recipe in 1967. Warm and fragrant, the succulent mushrooms rarely last long.

- **20** **medium-size mushrooms (about 1 lb. *total*)**
- **¾** **cup (¼ lb. plus ¼ cup) butter or margarine, at room temperature**
- **2** **cloves garlic, minced or pressed**
- **6** **tablespoons shredded jack cheese**
- **¼** **cup dry white or red wine**
- **2** **teaspoons soy sauce**
- **⅔** **cup fine cracker crumbs**

Remove and discard stems from mushrooms. Melt ¼ cup of the butter; brush over mushroom caps, coating thoroughly. In a medium-size bowl, combine remaining ½ cup butter, garlic, and cheese; stir until well blended. Stir in wine, soy sauce, and crumbs.

Place mushrooms, cavity side up, on a large rimmed baking sheet. Evenly mound filling in each mushroom, pressing it in lightly. Broil about 6 inches below heat until bubbly and lightly browned (about 3 minutes). Serve warm. Makes 20 appetizers.

Per appetizer: 86 calories (82 percent from fat), 1 g protein, 3 g carbohydrates, 8 g total fat (4 g saturated fat), 20 mg cholesterol, 143 mg sodium

Dry-roasted Potato Chips

Long baking in a low oven produces chips just as crisp as the familiar deep-fried kind. See page 9 for dip ideas.

- **1** **pound white thin-skinned potatoes, scrubbed**
- **2** **quarts water**
- **Vegetable oil cooking spray**
- **Salt**

Using a food slicer or food processor, cut potatoes into very thin slices. In a 3- to 4-quart pan, bring water to a boil. Add a third of the potatoes; cook until slightly translucent (about 1½ minutes). Lift out with a slotted spoon; drain on paper towels. Repeat to cook and drain remaining potato slices.

Place wire racks on large baking sheets (you'll need about 4 sheets to bake chips all at once). Lightly coat racks with cooking spray.

Arrange potato slices on racks in a single layer. Season to taste with salt. Bake in a 200° oven until chips are crisp (2 to 2½ hours). Serve hot or at room temperature. If made ahead, let cool; store airtight for up to 1 week. Makes about 4 cups.

Per ½ cup: 48 calories (7 percent from fat), 1 g protein, 10 g carbohydrates, 0.4 g total fat (0 g saturated fat), 0 mg cholesterol, 4 mg sodium

Hasty Hots

Among the simplest of our recipes, this ever-popular appetizer dates from *Sunset*'s earliest years.

- **4** **green onions, very thinly sliced**
- **½** **cup grated Parmesan cheese**
- **6** **to 8 tablespoons mayonnaise**
- **24** **slices cocktail-size rye bread or 24 baguette slices**

In a small bowl, stir together onions, cheese, and 6 tablespoons of the mayonnaise until well blended. If needed, add more mayonnaise to give mixture a firm spreading consistency. Place bread in single layer on a baking sheet; broil 4 to 6 inches below heat until golden brown. Turn slices over and spread with cheese mixture. Return to oven and broil until bubbly and lightly browned (about 3 minutes). Makes 2 dozen appetizers.

Per appetizer: 54 calories (61 percent from fat), 1 g protein, 4 g carbohydrates, 4 g total fat (0.9 g saturated fat), 4 mg cholesterol, 93 mg sodium

Roasted Potatoes with Asiago Cheese

Asiago, a hard Italian cheese with a rich, nutty flavor, is a winning complement for robust roasted potatoes.

- **16** **tiny red thin-skinned potatoes (*each* 1½ to 2 inches in diameter), scrubbed**
- **½** **cup grated Asiago or Parmesan cheese**
- **½** **cup mayonnaise**
- **2** **tablespoons thinly sliced green onion**
- **About 1 teaspoon paprika**

Pierce each potato in several places with a fork. Place potatoes in a baking pan and bake in a 375° oven until tender throughout when pierced (about 1 hour). Let cool; if baked ahead, cover and refrigerate until next day.

In a small bowl, mix cheese, mayonnaise, and onion. Cut each potato in half. Scoop a small (about ½-inch-deep) cavity in each potato half. Set halves, cut side up, in a 10- by 15-inch rimmed baking pan (if needed, trim a sliver off rounded sides of potato halves so they rest steadily). Spoon cheese mixture equally into each potato half. Dust liberally with paprika. Bake potatoes in a 350° oven until heated through (about 15 minutes). Serve hot. Makes 32 appetizers.

Per appetizer: 55 calories (53 percent from fat), 1 g protein, 5 g carbohydrates, 3 g total fat (0.7 g saturated fat), 3 mg cholesterol, 50 mg sodium

SOUPS, SALADS & SANDWICHES

Any time you want a simple meal—a quick lunch, a light supper, a patio picnic, or a late-night snack—turn to these pages for delicious soups, salads, and sandwiches. Many of the soup recipes incorporate seasonal or ethnic ingredients, yet most maintain the simplicity that has made soup a quintessential comfort food. The salads we offer, from satisfying entrées to colorful side-dish compositions of vegetables and greens, are both classic and contemporary. (We've lightened up your favorite dressings to serve alongside.) And some of our best traditional sandwiches, along with more modern fare, are worthy of main-dish status. Casual and fresh-flavored, these recipes showcase the international influences and the wealth of produce which have shaped our Western cuisine.

Italian Sausage Soup

Serve this chunky sausage soup with crisp breadsticks, a big green salad, and a carafe of red wine.

1½ pounds mild Italian sausages, cut into ½-inch-thick slices
2 cloves garlic, minced or pressed
2 large onions, chopped
1 large can (about 28 oz.) Italian-seasoned tomatoes
3 cans (about 14½ oz. *each*) beef broth
1½ cups dry red wine or water
½ teaspoon dry basil
3 tablespoons chopped parsley
1 medium-size green bell pepper, seeded and chopped
2 medium-size zucchini, cut into ½-inch-thick slices
3 cups (about 5 oz.) dry pasta bow ties
Grated Parmesan cheese

Cook sausage slices in a deep 5-quart pan over medium-high heat, stirring often, until lightly browned. Lift out sausage with a slotted spoon and set aside. Discard all but 3 tablespoons of the fat from pan. Add garlic and onions to pan; cook over medium heat, stirring often, until onions are soft (about 5 minutes).

Cut up tomatoes; then add tomatoes and their liquid to pan. Add sausage slices, broth, wine, and basil; stir to combine. Bring to a boil; then reduce heat, cover, and simmer for 20 minutes. Stir in parsley, bell pepper, zucchini, and pasta. Cover and simmer, stirring occasionally, until pasta and zucchini are tender to bite (10 to 15 minutes). Skim and discard fat from soup.

To serve, ladle soup into bowls; offer cheese to add to taste. Makes 6 servings.

Per serving: 505 calories (50 percent from fat), 24 g protein, 39 g carbohydrates, 28 g total fat (9 g saturated fat), 69 mg cholesterol, 2,020 mg sodium

Western Shellfish Bourride

Despite its name, this knife-and-fork soup is actually more akin to the tomato-based Italian-style *cioppino* than to the seafood *bourride* of southern France. The Western accent comes from meaty Dungeness crab and small Pacific oysters.

Vegetable Clam Stock (recipe follows)
¼ cup butter or margarine
¾ pound mushrooms, sliced
1 small jar (about 2 oz.) sliced pimentos, drained
24 to 36 small hard-shell clams, scrubbed; or 2 medium-size live or cooked Dungeness crabs (1½ to 2 lbs. *each*), cracked; or some of each
2 pounds halibut or lingcod steaks or fillets
1 pound medium-size raw shrimp, shelled and deveined
1 jar (about 10 oz.) small Pacific oysters, drained
Buttered toasted French bread slices
Grated Parmesan cheese

Prepare Vegetable Clam Stock. Bring to a simmer over medium-low heat.

Melt butter in a wide frying pan over medium heat; add mushrooms and cook, stirring occasionally, until soft (about 5 minutes). Add mushrooms, pimentos, and uncooked crab (if used) to simmering Vegetable Clam Stock; simmer, uncovered, for 5 minutes. Add clams (if used); simmer for 10 more minutes. Meanwhile, remove any skin and bones from fish; rinse fish, pat dry, and cut into pieces about 2 inches square. Add to stock; simmer for 2 more minutes. Add shrimp, oysters, and cooked crab (if used). Simmer until shrimp are opaque in center; cut to test (about 3 minutes).

To serve, ladle soup into shallow bowls. Serve with bread and cheese. Makes 8 to 10 servings.

Vegetable Clam Stock. Heat ¼ cup **olive oil** in a deep 8-quart pan over medium heat. Add 1 cup chopped **onion;** cook, stirring often, until golden (about 7 minutes). Add 5 cloves **garlic** (minced or pressed) and ⅓ cup minced **carrot;** cook, stirring often, until lightly browned. Coarsely chop tomatoes from 2 large cans (about 28 oz. *each*) **tomatoes;** stir in tomatoes and their liquid, 3 bottles (about 8 oz. *each*) **clam juice,** 1½ cups **dry white wine,** 2 dry **bay leaves,** ⅛ teaspoon crushed **fennel seeds,** ¼ cup chopped **parsley,** ½ teaspoon *each* **salt** and **pepper,** ¼ teaspoon **dry thyme,** and ¼ teaspoon **saffron threads,** if desired. Bring to a boil; then reduce heat, cover, and simmer for 15 minutes. If made ahead, let cool; then cover and refrigerate for up to 2 days.

Per serving: 402 calories (38 percent from fat), 42 g protein, 16 g carbohydrates, 16 g total fat (5 g saturated fat), 142 mg cholesterol, 817 mg sodium

TRADER GIOTTO'S
Tortellini & Chicken Soup

Succulent cheese-filled tortellini and chunks of tender chicken add heartiness to this homey favorite.

- **1 pound skinless, boneless chicken breasts**
- **4½ quarts or 3 large cans (about 49½ oz. *each*) chicken broth**
- **1 package (about 9 oz.) fresh or 6 ounces dried cheese-filled spinach tortellini**
- **1 pound spinach, rinsed well, stems removed, and leaves coarsely chopped**
- **½ pound mushrooms, sliced**
- **1 medium-size red bell pepper, seeded and diced**
- **1 cup cooked rice**
- **2 teaspoons dry tarragon**
  Grated Parmesan cheese (optional)

Rinse chicken, pat dry, and cut into ½-inch chunks. Set aside.

Pour broth into an 8- to 10-quart pan; cover and bring to a boil over high heat. Add tortellini; reduce heat to medium and boil gently, uncovered, just until tortellini are tender to bite (about 6 minutes). Add chicken, spinach, mushrooms, bell pepper, rice, and tarragon; return to a boil over high heat. Reduce heat, cover, and simmer until chicken is no longer pink in center; cut to test (about 2 minutes).

To serve, ladle soup into bowls; offer cheese. Makes 10 to 12 servings.

Per serving: 197 calories (19 percent from fat), 20 g protein, 20 g carbohydrates, 4 g total fat (0.2 g saturated fat), 37 mg cholesterol, 1,773 mg sodium

Curried Carrot-Peanut Soup

Pungent curry and creamy peanut butter lend Indian and Southeast

Asian accents to this savory vegetable soup. For a fresh-tasting foil for the rich, nutty flavors, stir in broccoli florets at the end of the cooking time.

- **1 pound carrots, chopped**
- **6 cups chicken broth**
- **½ cup finely chopped onion**
- **¼ cup creamy peanut butter**
- **1 clove garlic, minced or pressed**
- **2 tablespoons curry powder**
- **¼ cup rice**
- **2 cups (about 6 oz.) small broccoli florets**

In a 4- to 5-quart pan, combine carrots and 3 cups of the broth. Bring to a boil over high heat; then reduce heat to medium, cover, and boil gently until carrots are very tender to bite (25 to 30 minutes). Drain carrots, reserving broth.

In a blender or food processor, whirl carrots until smoothly puréed. Return purée to pan; add reserved cooking broth and stir until blended. Stir in remaining 3 cups broth, onion, peanut butter, garlic, curry powder, and rice. Bring to a boil over high heat; reduce heat, cover, and simmer, stirring occasionally, until rice is tender to bite (30 to 40 minutes). Add broccoli; cook just until tender when pierced (about 5 minutes). To serve, ladle soup into bowls. Makes 6 servings.

Per serving: 172 calories (37 percent from fat), 9 g protein, 20 g carbohydrates, 7 g total fat (0.9 g saturated fat), 0 mg cholesterol, 1,072 mg sodium

Western Classic
Spring Garden Soup

Abundant with fresh spring vegetables, this soup is often included in our readers' lists of favorites: it's pretty to look at, simple to prepare, and tastes delicious. For an easy light supper, serve it with crusty French bread and assorted cheeses.

- **¼ cup butter or margarine**
- **2 cups diced carrots**
- **1 large can (about 49½ oz.) chicken broth**
- **2 cups (about ¾ lb.) thinly sliced asparagus**
- **½ cup thinly sliced green onions**
- **1 to 2 cups shelled green peas or 1 package (about 10 oz.) frozen peas, thawed**
- **¼ cup minced parsley**
  Salt and pepper

Melt butter in a deep 5-quart pan over medium-low heat. Add carrots and cook, stirring often, until tender-crisp to bite (5 to 7 minutes). Add broth and bring to a boil over high heat. Add asparagus, onions, and peas. Reduce heat to medium-low, cover, and simmer until asparagus is tender to bite (about 5 minutes). Stir in parsley. Season to taste with salt and pepper.

To serve, ladle soup into bowls or mugs. Makes 8 to 10 servings.

Per serving: 106 calories (51 percent from fat), 5 g protein, 9 g carbohydrates, 6 g total fat (3 g saturated fat), 14 mg cholesterol, 742 mg sodium

Thai Pomelo & Shrimp Salad

The pomelo is a large Asian winter citrus fruit. It's round or pear-shaped, with smooth yellow skin and pink or white flesh. The flesh is slightly sweeter than grapefruit; the skin and pith are bitter.

    Tart-Hot Dressing (recipe follows)
3   **tablespoons sweetened shredded or flaked coconut**
1   **tablespoon salad oil**
2   **large cloves garlic, peeled and thinly sliced**
1   **large pomelo (about 2½ lbs.)**
⅓   **pound small cooked shrimp**
¼   **cup thinly sliced shallots**
    Butter or green leaf lettuce leaves, rinsed and crisped
¼   **cup salted peanuts, chopped**
    Cilantro sprigs

Prepare Tart-Hot Dressing; set aside.

Toast coconut in a small frying pan over low heat, stirring often, until golden (5 to 8 minutes). Pour out of pan and set aside. Add oil and garlic to pan. Stir over medium heat just until garlic is golden brown and crisp (2 to 3 minutes); set aside.

Peel pomelo and remove pith and membranes. Separate segments, then gently pull segments apart to separate the tiny juice sacs (firm, dry-textured fruit segments separate easily; if fruit does not do this readily, leave the segments whole). In a bowl, gently mix shredded pomelo (do not mix in whole segments; set aside), shrimp, shallots, and dressing.

To serve, line 4 salad or dinner plates with lettuce. Spoon equal portions of shredded pomelo salad onto lettuce. (If using whole segments, arrange equal portions of segments on lettuce; spoon shrimp mixture over fruit.) Garnish salads equally with coconut, garlic, peanuts, and cilantro sprigs. Makes 4 servings.

Tart-Hot Dressing. In a small bowl, whisk together 2 tablespoons **lime juice,** 2 tablespoons **fish sauce** (*nuoc mam* or *nam pla*) or soy sauce, 1 tablespoon minced **fresh ginger,** 1 teaspoon **sugar,** and ½ to ¾ teaspoon **crushed red pepper flakes.**

Per serving: 243 calories (37 percent from fat), 13 g protein, 27 g carbohydrates, 10 g total fat (2 g saturated fat), 73 mg cholesterol, 172 mg sodium

Spinach Salad with Pine Nut Dressing

Tossed with toasted pine nuts and a hint of lemon, fresh spinach takes on a Mediterranean flavor.

⅔   **cup pine nuts or slivered almonds**
7   **tablespoons olive oil or salad oil**
2½ **tablespoons wine vinegar**
⅛   **teaspoon ground nutmeg**
½   **teaspoon *each* grated lemon peel and dry tarragon**
1½ **pounds spinach, rinsed well, stems removed**
    Salt

Spread pine nuts in a shallow baking pan and toast in a 350° oven, stirring occasionally, until lightly browned (5 to 8 minutes). Let cool.

In a bowl, combine pine nuts, oil, vinegar, nutmeg, lemon peel, and tarragon. Cover and let stand at room temperature for at least 30 minutes or until next day.

To serve, select large leaves from spinach and use to line 8 salad plates. Cut remaining leaves into thin slivers; mound on plates. Stir dressing to blend, then drizzle over salads. Season to taste with salt. Makes 8 servings.

Per serving: 181 calories (82 percent from fat), 5 g protein, 4 g carbohydrates, 18 g total fat (3 g saturated fat), 0 mg cholesterol, 50 mg sodium

Olive-Pecan Chicken Slaw

Tender chunks of chicken, toasted pecans, and crunchy apple add up to an ideal light supper or lunch.

2   **teaspoons butter or margarine**
½   **cup pecans**
    Mustard Cream Dressing (recipe follows)
2   **cups shredded cabbage**
1½ **cups cubed cooked chicken breast**
1   **medium-size Red Delicious apple, cored and diced**
1   **can (about 2¼ oz.) sliced ripe olives, drained**
1   **small jar (about 2 oz.) diced pimentos, drained**
¼   **cup thinly sliced celery**
    Salt

Melt butter in a wide frying pan over medium heat. Add pecans and cook, stirring often, until nuts turn a darker brown (about 7 minutes). Drain on paper towels.

Prepare Mustard Cream Dressing. Add cabbage, chicken, apple, olives, pimentos, and celery to dressing; toss to coat. Sprinkle pecans over salad; season with salt. Makes 6 servings.

Mustard Cream Dressing. In a serving bowl, stir together ½ cup **mayonnaise,** 2 tablespoons **lemon juice,** 1 teaspoon **Dijon mustard** or regular prepared mustard, ½ teaspoon **sugar,** and ¼ teaspoon **pepper.**

Per serving: 299 calories (72 percent from fat), 12 g protein, 9 g carbohydrates, 24 g total fat (4 g saturated fat), 44 mg cholesterol, 272 mg sodium

Light Dressings

Homemade dressings add flavor and richness to even the simplest combinations of fresh ingredients. And by making a few quick changes in the traditional recipes, you can streamline many of your old favorites.

Try Spicy French Dressing or Orange-Basil Vinaigrette as a light complement to fresh greens or seasonal fruits. You'll enjoy our lightened-up creamy dressings, too. Creamy Blue Cheese, Green Goddess, and Thousand Island dressings are as flavorful and smooth as the originals, but we cut the fat by using lowfat buttermilk and reduced-calorie mayonnaise.

Spicy French Dressing

- ½ cup *each* sugar and cider vinegar
- 1 tablespoon all-purpose flour
- 1 teaspoon *each* salt and Worcestershire
- 1 medium-size onion, finely chopped
- 1 clove garlic, minced or pressed
- 2 tablespoons salad oil or olive oil
- ⅓ cup catsup
- 1 teaspoon celery seeds

In a small pan, stir together sugar, vinegar, and flour. Cook over medium heat, stirring, until bubbly (about 5 minutes). In a blender or food processor, combine vinegar mixture, salt, Worcestershire, onion, and garlic; whirl until smooth. With blender on lowest speed, gradually pour in oil. Transfer dressing to a bowl and stir in catsup and celery seeds. If made ahead, cover and refrigerate for up to 1 month. Makes about 2 cups.

Per tablespoon: 25 calories (30 percent from fat), 0.1 g protein, 4 g carbohydrates, 0.9 g total fat (0.1 g saturated fat), 0 mg cholesterol, 100 mg sodium

Thousand Island Dressing

- 1 cup reduced-calorie or regular mayonnaise
- ¼ cup tomato-based chili sauce
- 2 teaspoons minced onion
- 1 tablespoon *each* minced green bell pepper and pimento
- 2 tablespoons sweet pickle relish
- 1 hard-cooked egg, finely chopped
  Salt and pepper
  Milk or half-and-half (optional)

In a small bowl, stir together mayonnaise, chili sauce, onion, bell pepper, pimento, pickle relish, and egg. Season to taste with salt and pepper. If desired, thin with a little milk. If made ahead, cover and refrigerate for up to 1 week. Makes about 1¾ cups.

Per tablespoon: 30 calories (74 percent from fat), 0.4 g protein, 2 g carbohydrates, 2 g total fat (0.6 g saturated fat), 10 mg cholesterol, 89 mg sodium

Creamy Blue Cheese Dressing

- ¾ cup lowfat buttermilk
- 2 tablespoons *each* chopped parsley, plain nonfat yogurt, white wine vinegar, and crumbled blue-veined cheese
- 1 teaspoon salad oil or olive oil
- 1 tablespoon minced shallot
  White pepper

In a blender or food processor, combine buttermilk, parsley, yogurt, vinegar, cheese, oil, and shallot; whirl until smooth. Season to taste with white pepper. If made ahead, cover and refrigerate for up to 1 week. Makes about 1 cup.

Per tablespoon: 13 calories (49 percent from fat), 0.7 g protein, 0.9 g carbohydrates, 0.7 g total fat (0.3 g saturated fat), 1 mg cholesterol, 28 mg sodium

Orange-Basil Vinaigrette

- 1 cup orange juice
- 2 teaspoons cornstarch
- ⅓ cup white wine vinegar
- 2 teaspoons *each* Dijon mustard and dry basil
- 2 teaspoons olive oil

In a small pan, combine orange juice and cornstarch; stir until cornstarch is dissolved. Bring to a boil over medium heat; boil, stirring, for 30 seconds. Pour into a small bowl and refrigerate until cold. Then whisk in vinegar, mustard, basil, and oil until blended. If made ahead, cover and refrigerate until next day. Makes about 1 cup.

Per tablespoon: 15 calories (36 percent from fat), 0.1 g protein, 2 g carbohydrates, 0.6 g total fat (0.1 g saturated fat), 0 mg cholesterol, 19 mg sodium

Green Goddess Buttermilk Dressing

- ⅓ cup lowfat buttermilk
- ¼ cup *each* sliced green onions, coarsely chopped parsley, and coarsely chopped watercress
- ½ teaspoon dry tarragon
- 2 teaspoons lemon juice
- ½ teaspoon anchovy paste
- ½ cup reduced-calorie or regular mayonnaise
  Salt and pepper

In a blender or food processor, combine buttermilk, onions, parsley, watercress, tarragon, lemon juice, and anchovy paste; whirl until herbs are finely chopped. Add mayonnaise; whirl just until blended. Season to taste with salt and pepper. If made ahead, cover and refrigerate for up to 10 days. Makes about 1 cup.

Per tablespoon: 24 calories (78 percent from fat), 0.3 g protein, 1 g carbohydrates, 2 g total fat (0.5 g saturated fat), 3 mg cholesterol, 54 mg sodium

Black Bean, Corn & Pepper Salad

In this spirited Mexican-style salad, fresh jalapeños lend a fiery kick to a cool combination of black beans, corn kernels, and red bell pepper.

- 2 cans (about 15 oz. *each*) black beans or cannellini (white kidney beans), drained and rinsed
- 1½ cups cooked fresh corn kernels; or 1 package (about 10 oz.) frozen corn kernels, thawed
- 1 large red bell pepper, seeded and diced
- 2 small fresh jalapeño chiles, seeded and minced
- ½ cup firmly packed chopped cilantro
- ¼ cup lime juice
- 2 tablespoons salad oil
  Salt and pepper
  Lettuce leaves, rinsed and crisped

In a large bowl, mix beans, corn, bell pepper, chiles, cilantro, lime juice, and oil. Season to taste with salt and pepper. Cover and refrigerate for at least 1 hour or until next day.

Serve in a salad bowl lined with lettuce leaves. Serve cold or at room temperature. Makes 6 servings.

Per serving: 193 calories (26 percent from fat), 9 g protein, 28 g carbohydrates, 6 g total fat (0.7 g saturated fat), 0 mg cholesterol, 186 mg sodium

Cucumbers in Sour Cream

Easy to prepare and deliciously simple, this salad is a long-time favorite.

- 3 large cucumbers, peeled and cut into ⅛-inch-thick slices
- 1 teaspoon salt
- 1 cup sour cream
- ⅓ cup mayonnaise

- 1 tablespoon tarragon wine vinegar
- 2 green onions, thinly sliced
- 1 tablespoon finely minced parsley
- 1 clove garlic, minced or pressed
- 1 teaspoon Worcestershire

In a bowl, stir together cucumbers and salt. Let stand for 15 minutes; drain well on paper towels.

In another bowl, stir together sour cream, mayonnaise, and vinegar. Stir in onions, parsley, garlic, and Worcestershire. Add cucumbers and stir. Cover and refrigerate for at least 2 hours. Serve cold. Makes 6 to 8 servings.

Per serving: 165 calories (81 percent from fat), 2 g protein, 6 g carbohydrates, 15 g total fat (6 g saturated fat), 21 mg cholesterol, 407 mg sodium

Western Classic
California Shrimp Salad

A lemony onion vinaigrette complements avocado and poached shrimp.

- 2 pounds medium-size raw shrimp
  Green Onion Dressing (recipe follows)
- 1 large avocado
- 1 large head iceberg lettuce, shredded

Bring a 4- to 5-quart pan of water to a boil over high heat. Add shrimp. Reduce heat and simmer, uncovered, until shrimp are just opaque in center; cut to test (4 to 5 minutes). Drain shrimp; then shell and devein.

Prepare Green Onion Dressing. Pit, peel, and cube avocado. Combine shrimp and avocado in a serving bowl. Pour dressing over avocado and shrimp; mix to coat well. Cover and refrigerate for 1 to 2 hours.

Arrange lettuce on a platter. With a slotted spoon, lift shrimp mixture from bowl (reserve dressing) and

mound on lettuce. Offer reserved dressing. Makes 6 to 8 servings.

Green Onion Dressing. In a small bowl, whisk together ¼ cup **olive oil** or salad oil, ¼ cup **white wine vinegar,** 2 tablespoons **lemon juice,** ½ teaspoon **garlic salt,** ⅛ teaspoon **seasoned pepper,** and ½ cup thinly sliced **green onions.**

Per serving: 259 calories (52 percent from fat), 23 g protein, 8 g carbohydrates, 15 g total fat (2 g saturated fat), 160 mg cholesterol, 301 mg sodium

OLIVE OIL

There are two methods to extract olive oil from the fruit: mechanical pressing and solvent extraction. Pressing requires less heat; hence the term "cold pressed." The best olive oils are mechanically pressed. *Extra Virgin Olive Oil*, the result of the first pressing of the olive, has less than 1% acidity and is always cold pressed; it is considered the finest and fruitiest olive oil. *Pure olive oil* is a blend of extra virgin olive oil and refined olive oil which has been heated and often chemically extracted. Extra virgin oil is added to refined oil for color and to enhance the flavor. The acidity level of pure olive oil is between 1.0 and 3.3%.

Merida Salad

This light, tart citrus salad, from the town of Merida on the Yucatán peninsula, is a delightful complement to spicy main dishes.

- 2 **large oranges**
- 2 **tangerines**
- 2 **large pink grapefruit**
- 2 **large green-skinned apples**
- ¼ **cup lime juice**
- **Salt**
- ½ **cup cilantro leaves**

Holding fruit over a bowl to catch juice, use a sharp knife to cut peel and all white membrane from oranges, tangerines, and grapefruit; then cut segments free. Core and thinly slice apples. Arrange fruit in a shallow serving dish and sprinkle with lime juice and any accumulated citrus juices. Season to taste with salt; garnish with cilantro. Makes 8 servings.

Per serving: 83 calories (4 percent from fat), 1 g protein, 21 g carbohydrates, 0.4 g total fat (0 g saturated fat), 0 mg cholesterol, 2 mg sodium

Niçoise Salad

If you see the word "Niçoise" in the name of a recipe, you know the dish is prepared in the style of Nice, France—and that means it probably includes tomatoes, olives, and anchovies. The classic Niçoise salad contains those ingredients, as well as sliced potatoes, tender green beans, tuna, and hard-cooked eggs.

- ¾ **cup olive oil or salad oil**
- ¼ **cup red wine vinegar**
- 2 **tablespoons thinly sliced green onion or snipped chives**
- 2 **tablespoons finely chopped parsley**
- **Salt and pepper**
- 4 **large thin-skinned potatoes (about 2 lbs. *total*), scrubbed**

- 1½ **pounds green beans, ends and strings removed**
- 2 **large tomatoes, cut into wedges**
- 2 **or 3 hard-cooked eggs, quartered**
- ½ **cup Niçoise olives or pitted ripe olives**
- 1 **tablespoon drained capers (optional)**
- **Butter lettuce leaves, rinsed and crisped**
- 1 **can (about 6⅛ oz.) water-packed solid-pack tuna**
- 10 **to 12 canned anchovy fillets, drained**

In a small bowl, whisk together oil, vinegar, onion, and parsley. Season to taste with salt and pepper, then cover and set aside.

Cook potatoes in boiling water until tender throughout when pierced (about 25 minutes). Drain, immerse in ice water until cool, and drain again. Peel and slice potatoes; place in a bowl and pour just enough dressing over slices to coat them. Mix gently, cover, and refrigerate for at least 2 hours.

Cut beans into 1½-inch lengths and cook in boiling water until tender-crisp to bite (about 7 minutes). Drain, immerse in ice water until cool, and drain again.

On a rimmed platter, arrange potatoes, beans, tomatoes, and eggs in separate mounds. Garnish with olives and capers, if desired. (At this point, you may cover and refrigerate for up to 6 hours.)

Just before serving, arrange lettuce leaves around edge of platter. Drain tuna (without removing it from can); then invert can on top of salad. Carefully lift off can. Garnish salad with anchovies; pour remaining dressing over all ingredients. Makes 4 servings.

Per serving: 752 calories (56 percent from fat), 27 g protein, 57 g carbohydrates, 48 g total fat (7 g saturated fat), 156 mg cholesterol, 770 mg sodium

Dilled Green Pea Salad

Green peas are an ideal foil for dill in this classic from the 1960s. Serve on lettuce-lined plates, garnished with wedges of hard-cooked egg.

- 2 **packages (about 10 oz. *each*) frozen peas**
- 3 **tablespoons salad oil**
- 1 **to 2 tablespoons lemon juice**
- ¾ **teaspoon dry dill weed**
- ¼ **teaspoon dry basil**
- 1 **clove garlic, peeled**
- **Salt and pepper**
- 1 **cup thinly sliced celery**
- 6 **large butter lettuce leaves, rinsed and crisped**
- 3 **hard-cooked eggs, quartered (optional)**

Cook peas according to package directions; drain, reserving ⅓ cup of the cooking water. In a large bowl, combine peas, the reserved ⅓ cup cooking water, oil, lemon juice, dill weed, basil, and garlic. Season to taste with salt and pepper. Cover and refrigerate for 1 hour. Discard garlic. Add celery and toss lightly.

To serve, place a lettuce leaf on each of 6 salad plates; top equally with pea mixture. Garnish each serving with 2 wedges of hard-cooked egg, if desired. Makes 6 servings.

Per serving: 139 calories (45 percent from fat), 5 g protein, 14 g carbohydrates, 7 g total fat (0.9 g saturated fat), 0 mg cholesterol, 125 mg sodium

TRADER GIOTTO'S
Focaccia Milano

Italian *focaccia* often features baked vegetables atop a springy mattress of olive oil-anointed dough. Use it to make open-face sandwiches; here, we offer eggplant, tomato, or onion toppings. Or leave plain and slice horizontally to use with your favorite sandwich filling. You can make the dough ahead and let it rise overnight in the refrigerator. Or save even more time and use purchased frozen bread dough.

Focaccia Dough (recipe follows); or 2 loaves (about 1 lb. *each*) frozen white bread dough, thawed and kneaded together

2 tablespoons olive oil

Vegetable Topping (choices and directions follow)

Salt and pepper

Prepare Focaccia Dough. Coat bottom of a 10- by 15-inch rimmed baking pan with 1 tablespoon of the oil.

Punch dough down and knead briefly on a lightly floured board. Roll dough out to a rectangle about ½ inch thick. Lift dough into pan; pat firmly out to pan edges. (If dough is too elastic, let rest for about 5 minutes, then continue.) Cover dough lightly and let rise in a warm place until almost doubled (about 45 minutes). While dough is rising, prepare Vegetable Topping of your choice.

Brush remaining 1 tablespoon oil lightly over dough. With your fingers, gently press dough down all over, forming dimples in surface. Also gently push dough to fit into corners of baking pan. Evenly cover dough with topping; sprinkle lightly with salt and pepper.

Bake focaccia in a 400° oven until well browned on edges and bottom (30 to 40 minutes). If the topping is browned before bread is done, cover loosely with foil for last 10 to 15 minutes of baking.

Serve hot, warm, or cool; to serve, cut into pieces. If made ahead, cover and let stand at room temperature for up to 8 hours. To reheat, cover loosely with foil and heat in a 350° oven until warm to the touch (10 to 15 minutes). Makes 12 servings.

Focaccia Dough. In a large bowl, combine 1 package **active dry yeast** and 1½ cups **warm water** (about 110°F); let stand until yeast is softened (about 5 minutes). Stir in ½ teaspoon **salt** and 2 tablespoons **olive oil.** Then add 2½ cups **all-purpose flour;** stir to blend. Beat with a dough hook of an electric mixer on medium speed until dough is glossy and elastic (3 to 5 minutes). Stir in 1⅓ cups more **all-purpose flour.**

To knead by hand, scrape dough onto a lightly floured board and knead until smooth and springy (about 10 minutes), adding more flour as needed to prevent sticking. Place dough in a greased bowl; turn over to grease top.

To knead with a dough hook, beat dough on medium speed until it pulls from sides of bowl and is springy (5 to 7 minutes); if dough is sticky, add more flour, 1 tablespoon at a time.

Cover bowl of dough kneaded by either method with plastic wrap; let dough rise in a warm place until doubled—about 45 minutes. (Or let rise in refrigerator until next day.)

Vegetable Topping. Choose one of the following.

Eggplant. Seed and coarsely chop 1 large **red bell pepper.** Cut 2 medium-size unpeeled **eggplants** (about 1 lb. *each*) into ¾-inch cubes. Place vegetables in a 10- by 15-inch rimmed baking pan. Mix in 3 tablespoons **olive oil;** spread vegetables out in an even layer. Bake in a 450° oven, stirring once, until eggplant is lightly browned and begins to soften (about 25 minutes).

Over dimpled dough, sprinkle 2 cups (about 8 oz.) shredded **mozzarella cheese.** Distribute eggplant mixture over cheese. After baking, sprinkle focaccia with 2 tablespoons chopped **Italian parsley.**

Per serving: 301 calories (37 percent from fat), 9 g protein, 39 g carbohydrates, 12 g total fat (4 g saturated fat), 15 mg cholesterol, 167 mg sodium

Tomato. Coat a 10- by 15-inch rimmed baking pan with 1 tablespoon **olive oil.** Cut 2 pounds large **pear-shaped (Roma-type) tomatoes** lengthwise into ½-inch-thick slices. Lay slices in baking pan in a single layer, overlapping slightly if necessary. Drizzle 2 tablespoons **olive oil** over tomatoes. Bake in a 450° oven until tomatoes look dry and pan juices have evaporated (about 25 minutes). Gently loosen tomatoes from pan with a wide spatula.

Evenly space tomatoes over dimpled dough. Sprinkle with 1 teaspoon *each* **dry basil** and **dry oregano.**

Per serving: 233 calories (33 percent from fat), 5 g protein, 34 g carbohydrates, 9 g total fat (1 g saturated fat), 0 mg cholesterol, 99 mg sodium

Onion. Cut 3 medium-size **onions** in half lengthwise, then slice ¼ inch thick and place in a 10- by 15-inch rimmed baking pan. Mix in 2 tablespoons **olive oil.** Bake in a 450° oven, stirring occasionally, until onions are soft but not browned (about 20 minutes). Stir in ¼ cup **golden raisins** and 1 tablespoon chopped, drained **canned anchovy fillets.** Scatter over dimpled dough.

Per serving: 235 calories (28 percent from fat), 5 g protein, 37 g carbohydrates, 7 g total fat (1 g saturated fat), 0.8 mg cholesterol, 149 mg sodium

Curried Tuna-Apple Sandwiches

Spicy and sweet flavors mingle temptingly in these out-of-the-ordinary tuna sandwiches. To make them, you combine the ingredients, then serve the mixture open-faced on raisin bread.

- ¼ **cup mayonnaise**
- ½ **teaspoon curry powder**
- ¼ **teaspoon garlic salt**
- **Dash of ground red pepper (cayenne)**
- 1 **tablespoon lemon juice**
- 1 **can (about 6.125 oz.) water-packed chunk-style tuna, drained and flaked**
- ¾ **cup chopped apple**
- ½ **cup finely chopped celery**
- ¼ **cup raisins**
- 2 **tablespoons thinly sliced green onion**
- 4 **slices raisin bread or whole wheat bread, lightly toasted and buttered**
- **Alfalfa sprouts (optional)**

In a bowl, stir together mayonnaise, curry powder, garlic salt, red pepper, and lemon juice. Add tuna, apple, celery, raisins, and onion; stir until blended.

Spread an equal portion of tuna mixture over each slice of bread. Top with alfalfa sprouts, if desired. Makes 4 servings.

Per serving: 265 calories (41 percent from fat), 14 g protein, 25 g carbohydrates, 12 g total fat (2 g saturated fat), 24 mg cholesterol, 446 mg sodium

Chicken Supper Sandwiches

Served hot from the oven and teamed with your favorite soup or salad, these easy-to-make sandwiches are perfect for a light supper.

- 4 **slices bacon, *each* cut in half crosswise**
- 1½ **cups sliced cooked chicken or turkey breast**
- 2 **English muffins, split, toasted, and buttered**
- 4 **slices mild red onion**
- 1 **large tomato, peeled and cut into 4 thick slices**
- ½ **cup shredded Cheddar cheese**

Partially cook bacon in a wide frying pan over medium heat to remove most of fat (bacon should still be limp). Lift out and drain on paper towels.

Arrange chicken over muffin halves. Top chicken on each muffin half with an onion slice, a tomato slice, and 2 tablespoons of the cheese. Then arrange 2 bacon pieces atop each half.

Place muffin halves in a rimmed baking pan. Broil about 6 inches below heat until cheese is bubbly and bacon is crisp (3 to 5 minutes). Serve sandwiches open-faced; eat with knife and fork. Makes 2 servings.

Per serving: 634 calories (50 percent from fat), 46 g protein, 32 g carbohydrates, 35 g total fat (14 g saturated fat), 144 mg cholesterol, 742 mg sodium

Western Classic
Chile- & Cheese-stuffed Burgers

Devotion to the all-American all-meat hamburger may waver in favor of

this mildly spicy stuffed variation. What appears to be an ordinary beef patty contains a surprise filling of pickled jalapeño chiles and Cheddar cheese.

- 1½ **pounds lean ground beef**
- 3 **ounces Cheddar cheese, cut into matchstick-size pieces**
- 2 **to 3 tablespoons minced pickled jalapeño chiles**
- **Pepper and garlic salt**
- 4 **round sourdough French rolls (*each* about 4 inches in diameter) or hamburger buns, split**
- **Mayonnaise**
- **Green leaf lettuce leaves, rinsed and crisped**
- **Sliced tomatoes**

Divide beef into 8 equal portions; shape each portion into a ¼-inch-thick patty. Top 4 of the patties with equal amounts of the cheese and chiles; cover with remaining patties and press edges together to seal. Sprinkle both sides of each patty lightly with pepper and garlic salt.

Place patties on a lightly greased grill 4 to 6 inches above a solid bed of hot coals. Cook, turning once, until well browned on both sides and done to your liking; cut to test (10 to 12 minutes for medium-rare). When you turn patties over, place rolls, cut side down, around outside of grill to toast. Serve patties on rolls. Offer mayonnaise, lettuce, and tomatoes to add to taste. Makes 4 servings.

Per serving: 571 calories (50 percent from fat), 40 g protein, 30 g carbohydrates, 31 g total fat (14 g saturated fat), 127 mg cholesterol, 648 mg sodium

Up-to-date spreads get a lively boost from a variety of herbs, spices, and seasonal vegetables. Ranging from mild and creamy to spicy and chunky, the choices on this page bring savory flavors—and delicious contrasts in texture—to all kinds of sandwiches.

Classic Pesto

- 2 cups lightly packed fresh basil leaves
- 1 cup (about 4 oz.) grated Parmesan cheese
- ¼ cup olive oil
- 2 tablespoons pine nuts
- 1 or 2 cloves garlic

In a food processor or blender, combine basil, cheese, oil, pine nuts, and garlic; whirl until puréed. If made ahead, cover and refrigerate until next day. Bring to room temperature before using. Makes about 1 cup.

Per tablespoon: 75 calories (70 percent from fat), 4 g protein, 2 g carbohydrates, 6 g total fat (2 g saturated fat), 6 mg cholesterol, 133 mg sodium

Easy Guacamole

- 2 large ripe avocados
- 2 to 3 tablespoons lemon or lime juice
- 1 clove garlic, minced or pressed
- 1 to 2 tablespoons chopped cilantro
- 2 to 4 tablespoons canned diced green chiles
- 1 medium-size tomato, peeled, seeded, and chopped
  Minced fresh jalapeño or serrano chiles (optional)
  Salt
  Tortilla chips or crisp raw vegetables

Pit avocados and scoop pulp into a bowl; mash coarsely with a fork. Stir in lemon juice, garlic, cilantro, green chiles, and tomato. Add jalapeño chiles to taste, if desired. Season to taste with salt. Makes about 1⅔ cups.

Per tablespoon: 33 calories (75 percent from fat), 0.4 g protein, 2 g carbohydrates, 3 g total fat (0.5 g saturated fat), 0 mg cholesterol, 9 mg sodium

Homemade Mayonnaise

- 1 large egg or 3 egg yolks
- 1 teaspoon Dijon mustard
- 1 tablespoon white wine vinegar or lemon juice
- 1 cup salad oil or olive oil
  Salt (optional)

In a blender or food processor, combine egg, mustard, and vinegar. Whirl until well blended (3 to 5 seconds). With motor running, add oil in a slow, steady stream, whirling until mixture is smoothly blended. Season to taste with salt, if desired. If made ahead, cover and refrigerate for up to 2 weeks. Makes about 1½ cups.

Per tablespoon: 84 calories (98 percent from fat), 0.3 g protein, 0.1 g carbohydrates, 9 g total fat (1 g saturated fat), 9 mg cholesterol, 9 mg sodium

Egg-safe Mayonnaise

Mix 1 **egg white** with 2 tablespoons **lemon juice.** Cover airtight and refrigerate for at least 48 hours or up to 4 days (upon longer standing, egg begins to solidify). In a blender or food processor, whirl acidified egg white with 2 tablespoons **water** and 2 teaspoons **Dijon mustard.** With motor running, add 1 cup **salad oil** or olive oil in a slow, steady stream, whirling until mixture is smoothly blended. Season to taste with **lemon juice** and **salt;** whirl until blended. If made ahead, cover and refrigerate for up to 4 days. Makes about 1¼ cups.

Per tablespoon: 98 calories (99 percent from fat), 0.2 g protein, 0.2 g carbohydrates, 11 g total fat (1 g saturated fat), 0 mg cholesterol, 18 mg sodium

Green Mayonnaise

In a small bowl, combine 8 **watercress sprigs,** 6 to 10 **spinach leaves,** and 5 **parsley sprigs;** cover with **boiling water** and let stand for about 5 minutes. Drain, rinse with cold water, and drain again, pressing out excess moisture. Transfer greens to a blender or food processor. Add 2 teaspoons **lemon juice;** whirl until greens are finely minced. Then follow directions for **Homemade Mayonnaise** or Egg-safe Mayonnaise, adding egg, mustard, and vinegar to blender with minced greens. Makes about 1½ cups.

Per tablespoon: 84 calories (98 percent from fat), 0.3 g protein, 0.1 g carbohydrates, 9 g total fat (1 g saturated fat), 9 mg cholesterol, 10 mg sodium

Chipotle Chile Mayonnaise

Prepare **Homemade Mayonnaise** or Egg-safe Mayonnaise. Then add 3 **canned chipotle chiles in adobo sauce,** minced, and 1 tablespoon **sauce from chiles** to mayonnaise in blender. Whirl until chiles are finely minced. Makes about 1½ cups.

Per tablespoon: 89 calories (94 percent from fat), 0.3 g protein, 1 g carbohydrates, 9 g total fat (1 g saturated fat), 9 mg cholesterol, 46 mg sodium

*F*ew ingredients complement each other as perfectly as eggs and cheese, so it's no wonder that this simple combination is favored the world over as a base for both savory and sweeter dishes. ● This chapter presents a collection of long-time favorites—most featuring both eggs and cheese, some starring just one of the duo. We've included traditional Swiss fondue, a light and airy cheese soufflé, some very special pancakes, and a variety of international specialties. From Spain comes the classic tortilla. Italy gives us the crusty, golden brown torta rustica. Mexico offers spicy enchiladas and a not-too-spicy quiche. All in all, you'll find plenty of ideas for breakfast, brunch, lunch, or supper.

Mexican Quiche

In 1980, we offered this crustless Mexican-spiced interpretation of the classic French quiche. Chunks of chorizo sausage, mild green chiles, and whole kernels of corn give the tender jack cheese custard a south-of-the-border flair.

> **About 1 pound chorizo sausages, casings removed**
> 2 **medium-size onions, chopped**
> 1 **teaspoon salt**
> ⅛ **teaspoon pepper**
> ¼ **cup diced fresh mild green chiles or canned diced green chiles**
> 10 **eggs**
> 2 **cups milk or half-and-half**
> 1 **can (about 2¼ oz.) sliced ripe olives, drained**
> 1 **can (about 8¾ oz.) whole-kernel corn, drained**
> 3 **cups (about 12 oz.) shredded jack cheese**
> **Avocado and tomato slices**
> **Cilantro sprigs**

Crumble chorizo into a wide frying pan and cook over medium-high heat, stirring often, until browned. Add onions and cook, stirring often, until soft (about 4 minutes). Discard fat. Stir in salt, pepper, and chiles. Remove from heat.

In a large bowl, beat eggs and milk until blended. Stir in chorizo mixture, olives, corn, and cheese. Evenly spread mixture in a greased 10- by 15-inch rimmed baking pan.

Bake in a 375° oven until a knife inserted in center comes out clean (25 to 30 minutes). Let stand for 10 minutes before serving. To serve, cut into squares and garnish with avocado, tomato, and cilantro sprigs. Makes 6 to 8 servings.

Per serving: 549 calories (62 percent from fat), 33 g protein, 19 g carbohydrates, 38 g total fat (8 g saturated fat), 395 mg cholesterol, 1,093 mg sodium

Spanish Tortilla

In Spain, a *tortilla* is a pepper-studded egg-and-potato dish. It's served as a snack or light supper with sherry.

> 3 **tablespoons olive oil**
> 1 **small onion, finely chopped**
> 2 **cloves garlic, minced or pressed**
> 2 **medium-size thin-skinned potatoes, scrubbed and cut into ¼-inch cubes**
> 1 **can (about 6 oz.) pitted ripe olives, drained**
> 1 **jar (about 7 oz.) roasted red peppers, drained; or 1 large can (about 7 oz.) diced green chiles**
> 9 **eggs**
> **Sour cream (optional)**

Heat 1 tablespoon of the oil in a wide nonstick frying pan over medium heat. Add onion and garlic; cook, stirring often, just until onion is soft (about 5 minutes). Add remaining 2 tablespoons oil, then potatoes; turn with a wide spatula to coat potatoes evenly with oil. Cook over medium-high heat, turning often, until potatoes are golden and tender to bite (about 15 minutes). Coarsely chop olives and peppers; stir into potato mixture.

In a large bowl, beat eggs until blended. Reduce heat under potatoes to low; add eggs. Cover and cook until eggs are set about 1 inch around pan edges but still look liquid in center (about 8 minutes). Uncover; tilt pan and, with a spatula, slightly lift edges of tortilla to let any uncooked egg flow underneath. Cover and cook until eggs are set but tortilla is still moist on top (5 to 10 minutes).

Ease spatula down sides and beneath tortilla to loosen it from pan. Invert a flat plate over pan. Protecting your hands, hold plate and pan together; invert both, then lift off pan. With a spatula, slide tortilla from plate back into pan, cooked side up. Cook, uncovered, until eggs are set on bottom; lift with spatula to test (about 1 minute). Slide tortilla onto a platter. Serve hot, warm, or at room temperature. To serve, cut into wedges. Offer sour cream. Makes 4 to 6 servings.

Per serving: 318 calories (59 percent from fat), 14 g protein, 19 g carbohydrates, 21 g total fat (4 g saturated fat), 383 mg cholesterol, 422 mg sodium

CHEESES

•

When assembling a cheese platter, it is best to offer at least three cheeses. Think of contrast in terms of taste, color, and texture and try to include examples from different "families" of cheeses. They include:

Hard	Romano, Parmesan, and other "grating-type" cheeses
Semi-firm	Cheddar, Swiss and French-type "holey" cheeses
Blues	All the blue-veined (including many soft-ripened) cheeses
Semisoft	Havarti, Fontina, and Münster.
Soft-Ripened	Brie, Camembert, and cheeses with at least 50% butterfat
Double & Triple cream	St. André, Brillat Savarin, and the creamy rich varieties with 60% (double) and 70–75% (triple) butterfat
Chevres	Pure goat's milk cheeses and goat's and cow's milk combinations

Serve cheese at room temperature in order to maximize flavor and texture.

Torta Rustica

Easy to pack and delicious served at any temperature, this traditional Northern Italian specialty is a perfect choice for a no-fuss picnic. Our recipe lets you exercise some creativity—you can take your pick from three fillings and two different shapes.

Torta Filling (choices and recipes follow)
1 **package (about 1 lb.) hot yeast roll mix, plus water, butter or margarine, and egg as specified on package**
1 **egg, lightly beaten**

Prepare Torta Filling; set aside.

Prepare hot yeast roll mix according to package directions; knead briefly on lightly floured board. Cut off a third of the dough; set aside. Roll out remaining portion to a 13-inch round; fit over bottom and up sides of a greased 9-inch spring-form pan. Cover evenly with filling.

Shape reserved dough as a lattice or wedges. *For lattice,* roll dough out to a 9-inch square and cut into strips about 1 inch wide. Weave strips over filling in a lattice pattern, tucking ends of dough down around filling at pan rim. *For wedges,* roll dough out to a 9-inch round; cut into 8 wedges. Arrange wedges side by side on filling, with tips meeting in center.

Lightly cover torta and let rise in a warm place until puffy (30 to 40 minutes). Uncover; brush top with egg.

Bake on lowest rack of a 350° oven until richly browned (35 to 40 minutes). Let cool in pan on a rack for about 5 minutes, then remove pan rim. Serve warm or at room temperature. If made ahead, let cool; then cover and refrigerate until next day. To reheat, wrap cold torta in foil and bake in a 350° oven for 40 minutes (it takes as long to reheat as to bake).

To serve, cut torta into wedges. Makes 6 to 8 servings.

Torta Filling. Choose one of the following.

Spinach & ricotta. In a bowl, combine 2 packages (about 10 oz. *each*) **frozen chopped spinach,** thawed and squeezed dry; 1 cup **ricotta cheese;** ½ cup grated **Parmesan cheese;** 1 **egg yolk;** ½ teaspoon **garlic salt;** and ⅛ teaspoon **pepper.** Stir until blended.

Per serving: 364 calories (32 percent from fat), 15 g protein, 47 g carbohydrates, 13 g total fat (7 g saturated fat), 122 mg cholesterol, 748 mg sodium

Tuna & cheese. Thinly slice 1 small **onion** and separate into rings. Heat 1 tablespoon **olive oil** in a small frying pan over medium heat. Add onion and ¼ cup finely chopped **green or red bell pepper;** cook, stirring, until onion is lightly browned (about 10 minutes). Remove from heat and add 1 can (about 6⅛ oz.) **chunk-style tuna,** drained and chopped, and ¼ teaspoon **dry oregano;** stir until blended. Season to taste with **salt.** Distribute filling over dough as directed; cover with 1 cup (about 4 oz.) shredded **fontina or jack cheese.**

Per serving: 398 calories (33 percent from fat), 19 g protein, 47 g carbohydrates, 15 g total fat (6 g saturated fat), 93 mg cholesterol, 682 mg sodium

Sausage & tomato. Remove casings from ¾ pound **mild Italian sausages.** Crumble meat into a wide frying pan and cook over medium heat, stirring often, until browned; remove from heat. Discard fat. Stir in ¼ cup finely chopped **parsley** and 2 tablespoons grated **Parmesan cheese.** Distribute filling over dough as directed, then top with ½ cup well-drained **canned sliced tomatoes** and 1 cup (about 4 oz.) shredded **mozzarella cheese.**

Per serving: 436 calories (39 percent from fat), 19 g protein, 47 g carbohydrates, 19 g total fat (8 g saturated fat), 111 mg cholesterol, 914 mg sodium

Chile-Egg Puff

Similar to a creamy frittata, this simple egg dish may be served as either an appetizer or a brunch entrée. For an appetizer, bake in mini-muffin pans.

5 **eggs**
1 **cup cottage cheese**
¼ **cup butter or margarine, melted and cooled**
¼ **cup all-purpose flour**
½ **teaspoon *each* baking powder and salt**
2 **cups (about 8 oz.) shredded jack cheese**
1 **small can (about 4 oz.) diced green chiles**

In a large bowl, beat eggs with an electric mixer until thick and lemon-colored. Stir in cottage cheese, butter, flour, baking powder, and salt. Then add cheese and chiles; stir just until combined.

If serving chile puff as a main dish, pour egg mixture into a greased 8-inch-square baking pan. Bake in a 350° oven until edges are lightly browned and center feels firm when lightly pressed (about 35 minutes). If serving as an appetizer, spoon egg mixture into tiny (about 1-inch) muffin pans, using about 1½ tablespoons egg mixture per pan; bake in a 350° oven until firm (15 to 18 minutes). Makes 6 to 8 main-dish servings or about 40 appetizers.

Per main-dish serving: 288 calories (68 percent from fat), 17 g protein, 6 g carbohydrates, 22 g total fat (6 g saturated fat), 204 mg cholesterol, 703 mg sodium

Our recipe for a giant-size Dutch baby has been a favorite for decades. The rich batter puffs dramatically in the oven. For the most impressive rise, use a large, shallow pan (be sure to adjust the amounts of ingredients to match pan size). Serve the pancake with your choice of toppings, for brunch or dessert. Griddle-baked cottage cheese pancakes are a great wake-up, too.

Dutch Baby Pancakes

Select pan of the appropriate size (see below). Place **butter** in pan and set in a 425° oven. While butter is melting, place **eggs** in a blender or food processor and whirl at high speed for 1 minute. With motor running, gradually pour in **milk,** then slowly add **flour;** continue whirling for 30 seconds. (Or, in a bowl, beat eggs until blended; gradually beat in milk, then flour.)

Remove pan from oven and pour in batter. Return pan to oven and bake until pancake is well browned and puffy (20 to 25 minutes, depending on pan size).

Dust pancake with **ground nutmeg,** if desired. To serve, cut into wedges; serve at once with any of the following toppings. Makes 3 to 6 servings.

Toppings. Choose one of the following; or create your own topping.

Pan Size	Butter or Margarine	Eggs	Milk & All-purpose Flour
2–3 qt.	2 tablespoons	3	¾ cup *each*
3–4 qt.	3 tablespoons	4	1 cup *each*
4–4½ qt.	¼ cup	5	1¼ cups *each*
4½–5 qt.	¼ cup	6	1½ cups *each*

Powdered sugar classic. Have a shaker or bowl of **powdered sugar** and thick wedges of **lemon** at the table. Sprinkle sugar on hot pancake; then squeeze lemon juice over all.

Fruit. Use your favorite **fresh fruit** (cored and sliced, if necessary) or canned fruit. Top pancake with fruit; drizzle with **honey** or dust with **powdered sugar.**

Hot fruit. Cook **apple or pear slices** in melted **butter** or margarine over medium heat until tender; spoon over pancake and offer with **sour cream** or plain yogurt. Or heat **banana or papaya slices** in melted **butter** or margarine over medium heat; spoon over pancake and serve with **lime wedges**.

Canned pie filling. Combine 1 can (about 21 oz.) **cherry or apple pie filling** with **lemon juice** and **ground cinnamon** to taste. Serve cold or warm over pancake; top with **plain yogurt.**

Syrups. Offer **maple syrup,** honey, or any favorite fruit sauce or topping such as Cherries Jubilee or applesauce.

Per serving (without topping): 302 calories (48 percent from fat), 12 g protein, 27 g carbohydrates, 16 g total fat (8 g saturated fat), 244 mg cholesterol, 181 mg sodium

Cinnamon Apple Dutch Baby

Melt 2 tablespoons **butter** or margarine in 2- to 3-quart baking pan over medium heat. Stir in 2 teaspoons **ground cinnamon** and 3 tablespoons **sugar.** Add 2 medium-size **tart apples** (such as Gravenstein, Pippin, or Granny Smith), peeled, cored, and sliced; cook, stirring, until apples begin to soften (about 5 minutes). Spray inside edge of baking pan with **vegetable oil cooking spray.** Place pan in a 425° oven for 5 minutes.

Then follow directions for 2- to 3-quart **Dutch Baby Pancake**, but omit butter. Instead, pour batter into pan with apples. Bake until pancake is well browned and puffy (15 to 20 minutes). To serve, dust with **powdered sugar;** cut into wedges. Makes 6 servings.

Per serving: 232 calories (44 percent from fat), 6 g protein, 27 g carbohydrates, 12 g total fat (6 g saturated fat), 131 mg cholesterol, 125 mg sodium

Cottage Cheese Pancakes

- 3 **eggs**
- 1 cup **small-curd cottage cheese**
- 2 tablespoons **salad oil**
- ¼ cup **all-purpose flour**
- ¼ teaspoon **salt**
  Maple syrup

In a small bowl, beat eggs with a wire whisk or an electric mixer until thick and lemon-colored. Press cottage cheese through a fine wire strainer into eggs. Add oil; stir until blended. Then stir in flour and salt.

Spoon 4-inch circles of batter onto a lightly greased hot griddle. Cook pancakes, turning once, until golden brown on both sides. Serve with syrup on the side. Makes 2 to 4 servings.

Per serving: 305 calories (65 percent from fat), 16 g protein, 10 g carbohydrates, 22 g total fat (5 g saturated fat), 223 mg cholesterol, 527 mg sodium

Curried Eggs with Shrimp Sauce

Blanketed with a creamy sauce of shrimp and cheese, curry-seasoned deviled eggs are rich and hearty.

- 8 hard-cooked eggs
- 1 teaspoon salt
- ½ teaspoon *each* curry powder and paprika
- ¼ teaspoon dry mustard
- 1½ tablespoons lemon juice
  Dash of Worcestershire
- 2 to 3 tablespoons sour cream
- 2 tablespoons butter or margarine
- 2 tablespoons all-purpose flour
- 2 cups milk
- 1 cup (about 4 oz.) shredded sharp Cheddar cheese
- 1 teaspoon Worcestershire
  Salt and pepper
- 2 cups small cooked shrimp

Cut eggs in half lengthwise; remove yolks. Place yolks in a bowl; add the 1 teaspoon salt, curry powder, paprika, mustard, lemon juice, and a dash of Worcestershire; mash with a fork until blended. Add sour cream; blend. Fill egg halves with yolk mixture and press halves together to make 8 whole eggs. Place in a greased 8- or 9-inch baking dish; set aside.

Melt butter in a small pan over medium heat. Stir in flour and cook, stirring, for 1 minute (do not brown). Remove from heat and gradually stir in milk. Return to heat and cook, stirring constantly, until sauce boils and thickens. Stir in cheese and the 1 teaspoon Worcestershire; stir until cheese is melted. Season to taste with salt and pepper. Add shrimp; stir to combine. Pour over eggs. Bake in a 350° oven until bubbly and heated (about 20 minutes). Makes 4 to 6 servings.

Per serving: 391 calories (60 percent from fat), 29 g protein, 9 g carbohydrates, 26 g total fat (13 g saturated fat), 481 mg cholesterol, 893 mg sodium

Viennese Eggs

These deviled eggs have become a classic. For an elegant presentation, use a pastry bag with a rosette tip to pipe the yolk mixture into the whites.

- 9 hard-cooked eggs
- ½ cup sour cream
  Salt
  Thin lime slices, cut into quarters
  About 1½ tablespoons black caviar

Cut eggs in half lengthwise and remove yolks, being careful not to tear whites. Place yolks in a bowl and mash to a smooth paste with a fork. Blend in sour cream and season to taste with salt. Spoon yolk mixture into whites (or force through a pastry bag fitted with a large rosette tip). Top each egg half with a quarter-slice of lime and about ¼ teaspoon of the caviar. If made ahead, cover loosely with plastic wrap and refrigerate until next day. Makes 1½ dozen deviled-egg halves.

Per egg half: 56 calories (68 percent from fat), 4 g protein, 0.8 g carbohydrates, 4 g total fat (2 g saturated fat), 117 mg cholesterol, 54 mg sodium

Green Chile & Cheese Pie

California green chiles lend a mild piquancy to this simple pie. The creamy creation is easy to make—just mix the chiles with eggs and plenty of jack and Cheddar cheeses, then bake in a flaky pastry shell.

- All-purpose Pastry (recipe follows)
- 1½ cups (about 6 oz.) shredded jack cheese
- 1 cup (about 4 oz.) shredded mild Cheddar cheese
- 1 small can (about 4 oz.) diced green chiles
- 3 eggs
- 1 cup milk or half-and-half
- ¼ teaspoon salt
- ⅛ teaspoon ground cumin

Prepare All-purpose Pastry. On a lightly floured board, roll out pastry; fit pastry into a 9- or 10-inch pie pan. Trim and flute edges; lightly prick bottom and sides of pie shell with a fork. Bake in a 400° oven just until pale golden (about 12 minutes); let cool slightly.

Sprinkle all the jack cheese and ½ cup of the Cheddar cheese over bottom of pie shell. Distribute chiles over cheese. In a bowl, beat eggs with milk, salt, and cumin; pour into pie shell. Sprinkle remaining ½ cup Cheddar cheese lightly over top.

Bake in a 325° oven until center of pie appears set when pan is gently shaken (about 40 minutes). Let stand for about 15 minutes before serving. Serve hot or cold; to serve, cut into wedges. Makes 6 servings.

All-purpose Pastry. In a food processor or a bowl, combine 1¼ cups **all-purpose flour** and 6 tablespoons cold **butter** or margarine, cut into chunks. Whirl (or cut with a pastry blender or 2 knives) until mixture resembles fine crumbs. Add 1 **egg** and whirl until pastry holds together—about 8 seconds. (Or mix with a fork until pastry holds together.) Shape into a ball.

Per serving: 458 calories (62 percent from fat), 20 g protein, 24 g carbohydrates, 31 g total fat (13 g saturated fat), 223 mg cholesterol, 654 mg sodium

Swiss Fondue

Classic Swiss fondues, like this one from a 1960 *Sunset* cook book, are delicious but never foolproof. For the most reliable results, use imported Swiss cheese and keep the heat moderate—high heat will make the cheese stringy and oily, while low heat will make it too thick for dipping.

1   clove garlic, peeled and halved
    About 2 cups dry white wine
4   cups (about 1 lb.) shredded Swiss, Emmenthaler, or Gruyère cheese
1   tablespoon cornstarch
3   tablespoons kirsch
    Salt and pepper
    Dash of ground nutmeg
1   loaf (about 1 lb.) French bread, cut into bite-size pieces

Rub garlic over bottom of a ceramic fondue pot or chafing dish; discard garlic. Add 2 cups of the wine and heat over low heat. Mix cheese with cornstarch.

When bubbles rise to surface of wine, add a handful of the cheese-cornstarch mixture; stir constantly until cheese is melted. Continue to add cheese mixture in handfuls, stirring after each addition until cheese is completely melted. When cheese mixture is smooth and starts to bubble lightly, gradually pour in kirsch, stirring constantly until blended. Season to taste with salt and pepper; stir in nutmeg. Keep warm over heat source (fondue should bubble slowly).

To serve, offer fondue forks or bamboo skewers to spear bread for dipping. If needed, pour a little warm wine into cheese to maintain correct consistency. Makes 8 servings.

Per serving: 410 calories (41 percent from fat), 21 g protein, 35 g carbohydrates, 17 g total fat (10 g saturated fat), 52 mg cholesterol, 496 mg sodium

Sour Cream Enchiladas

Sour cream is both filling and garnish for these enchiladas. Two tortillas, over-lapped and rolled, make each enchilada.

2   cups sour cream
1   cup sliced green onions
½   teaspoon ground cumin
4   cups (about 1 lb.) shredded Longhorn cheese
1   can (about 10 oz.) enchilada sauce
    Salad oil
12 corn tortillas
    Sour cream (optional)
    Sliced green onions (optional)

In a bowl, stir together the 2 cups sour cream, the 1 cup onions, cumin, and 1 cup of the cheese; set aside.

In a small frying pan, heat enchilada sauce over low heat; keep warm. In another small frying pan, heat ¼ inch of oil over medium heat; keep hot. Heat one tortilla at a time in oil until it blisters and becomes limp (a few seconds). Using tongs, lift tortilla from oil and dip it into heated sauce. Arrange tortillas 2 at a time in a 7- by 11-inch or 9-inch-square baking pan. Overlap 2 tortillas at one end of pan; allow part of one to extend over rim. Spread about 6 tablespoons of the sour cream filling down center of tortillas; fold the extending sections over filling to make one enchilada.

Repeat to fill remaining tortillas, placing them side by side and completely covering pan bottom. Sprinkle remaining 3 cups cheese over top.

Bake, uncovered, in a 375° oven until cheese is melted (about 20 minutes). Garnish with sour cream and onions, if desired. Makes 6 servings.

Per serving: 725 calories (68 percent from fat), 25 g protein, 33 g carbohydrates, 56 g total fat (28 g saturated fat), 113 mg cholesterol, 1,047 mg sodium

Cheese Soufflé

Soufflés will rise highest if you first let egg whites come to room temperature. Then, beat until firm, but still moist and not crumbly, before folding them into the yolk mixture.

3   tablespoons butter or margarine
3   tablespoons all-purpose flour
1   cup milk
    Dash of ground red pepper (cayenne)
¼   teaspoon dry mustard
1   cup (about 4 oz.) shredded Cheddar or Swiss cheese
    Salt
4   or 5 eggs, separated

Melt butter in a medium-size pan over medium heat. Stir in flour and cook, stirring, for 1 minute (do not brown). Remove from heat and gradually stir in milk; then add red pepper and mustard. Return to heat and cook, stirring until sauce boils and thickens. Add cheese; stir until melted. Season to taste with salt. Remove from heat and beat in egg yolks, one at a time.

In a small bowl, beat egg whites with an electric mixer or a wire whisk until they hold distinct but moist peaks. Stir about a fourth of the whites into cheese mixture, then carefully fold in remaining whites until blended.

Pour into a well-buttered 1½-quart soufflé dish or four to six 1-cup ramekins. Draw a circle on surface of soufflé batter about 1 inch from rim, using a spoon or the tip of a knife. Bake in a 375° oven until soufflé feels firm when lightly tapped and crack looks fairly dry (about 35 minutes for a 1½-quart soufflé dish; about 20 minutes for ramekins). Serve at once. Makes 4 to 6 servings.

Per serving: 280 calories (71 percent from fat), 13 g protein, 7 g carbohydrates, 22 g total fat (12 g saturated fat), 245 mg cholesterol, 307 mg sodium

VEGETABLES

*T*he West is a treasure trove of fresh garden vegetables. Whether simply prepared with a sprinkling of herbs or combined with sauce in a savory casserole, each season's jewels offer the cook myriad possibilities for delicious presentation. ● The recipes in this chapter, many contributed by our readers, are the time-honored favorites often reserved for potluck gatherings and special family dinners. Rich, hearty choices such as Asparagus Parmesan, Pecan-topped Sweet Potatoes, and Deviled Green Beans are among the most popular selections. The Green Vegetable Medley and Asparagus with Orange-Butter Sauce are among the lighter dishes we've included as well. ● If you're looking for something different to serve as a side dish, try Broccoli with Pine Nuts & Rice, Diced Potatoes in Soy Sauce, or one of the other satisfying recipes in these pages.

Green Vegetable Medley

Peas, lima beans, and green beans combine in this rich and creamy cheese-topped casserole. If you like, you can put it together a day ahead, then pop it in the oven half an hour before serving.

- 1 **package (about 10 oz.) frozen baby lima beans**
- 1 **package (about 9 oz.) frozen cut green beans**
- 2 **tablespoons butter or margarine**
- ¼ **cup finely chopped onion**
- 1 **tablespoon all-purpose flour**
- ½ **cup *each* sour cream and mayonnaise**
- ½ **teaspoon dry basil**
- 1 **package (about 10 oz.) frozen peas, thawed**
  Salt and pepper
- ¾ **cup shredded sharp Cheddar cheese**

Following package directions, cook lima beans and green beans separately in boiling water just until tender-crisp to bite; do not overcook. Drain, immerse in ice water until cool, and drain again.

Melt butter in a wide frying pan over medium heat. Add onion and cook, stirring often, until soft (about 5 minutes). Stir in flour and cook, stirring, for 1 minute (do not brown). Remove from heat and add sour cream, mayonnaise, and basil; stir until blended. Stir in lima beans, green beans, and peas. Season to taste with salt and pepper. Spoon into a 1½ -to 2-quart baking dish and sprinkle with cheese. (At this point, you may cover and refrigerate until next day.)

Bake, uncovered, in a 325° oven until heated through (about 20 minutes; about 30 minutes if refrigerated). Makes 10 to 12 servings.

Per serving: 209 calories (63 percent from fat), 6 g protein, 13 g carbohydrates, 15 g total fat (5 g saturated fat), 24 mg cholesterol, 175 mg sodium

---

Asparagus with Orange-Butter Sauce

Fresh asparagus cloaked in a rich, citrusy butter sauce is a fitting accompaniment to an elegant meal. Strips of orange peel, tied into tiny knots garnish the slender green spears.

- 2 **pounds asparagus**
- ½ **cup (¼ lb.) butter or margarine**
- ⅓ **cup minced shallots**
- 1¼ **teaspoons Dijon mustard**
- 1⅓ **cups orange juice**
  Strips of orange peel tied in knots; or orange slices (optional)

Snap off and discard tough ends of asparagus; peel stalks, if desired. In a wide frying pan, bring 1 inch of water to a boil over high heat. Add asparagus; cover and cook just until barely tender when pierced (about 5 minutes). Drain, transfer to a platter, and keep warm.

Melt 1 tablespoon of the butter in a small pan over medium heat. Add shallots and cook, stirring often, for 1 minute. Add mustard and orange juice. Bring to a boil over high heat; boil, stirring occasionally, until reduced to ⅔ cup. Reduce heat to low and add remaining 7 tablespoons butter all at once; cook, stirring constantly, until butter is melted and sauce is smooth. Spoon sauce over asparagus and garnish with orange peel, if desired. Makes 6 servings.

Per serving: 186 calories (72 percent from fat), 3 g protein, 11 g carbohydrates, 16 g total fat (10 g saturated fat), 41 mg cholesterol, 191 mg sodium

Asparagus Parmesan

Thinly sliced asparagus bakes until meltingly soft beneath an onion-cheese sauce lightly spiced with curry.

- 2½ **pounds asparagus**
- ¼ **cup butter or margarine**
- 2 **to 3 tablespoons thinly sliced green onions**
- ¼ **teaspoon curry powder**
- ½ **teaspoon salt**
- ⅓ **cup all-purpose flour**
- 2 **cups milk; or 1⅔ cups milk plus ⅓ cup dry white wine**
- ⅓ **cup grated Parmesan cheese**

Snap off and discard tough ends of asparagus; cut stalks into slanting slices. In a wide frying pan, boil 1 inch of water over high heat. Add asparagus; cover and cook just until tender-crisp (about 3 minutes). Drain.

Melt butter in a medium-size pan over medium heat. Add onions, curry powder, and salt; cook, stirring often, until onions are soft (about 5 minutes). Stir in flour and cook, stirring, for 1 minute (do not brown). Remove from heat and gradually stir in milk. Then return to heat and cook, stirring constantly, until sauce boils and thickens. Stir in asparagus. Pour mixture into a shallow baking dish and sprinkle with cheese. Bake in a 400° oven until bubbly and heated through (15 to 20 minutes). Makes 6 to 8 servings.

Per serving: 159 calories (56 percent from fat), 7 g protein, 11 g carbohydrates, 10 g total fat (6 g saturated fat), 30 mg cholesterol, 330 mg sodium

Deviled Green Beans

This recipe from the 1950s gets plenty of flavor from Cheddar cheese, mustard, and garlic.

- 1 package (about 9 oz.) frozen cut green beans
- 3 tablespoons butter or margarine
- 1 medium-size onion, chopped
- 1 clove garlic, minced or pressed
- ½ green bell pepper, seeded and chopped
- 2 bottled pimentos, sliced or chopped
- 2 teaspoons prepared mustard
- 1 can (about 8 oz.) tomato sauce
- 1 cup (about 4 oz.) shredded Cheddar cheese

Following package directions, cook beans in boiling water until tender-crisp to bite. Drain, immerse in ice water until cool, and drain again.

Melt butter in a medium-size frying pan over medium heat. Add onion, garlic, bell pepper, and pimentos; cook, stirring often, until onion is soft (about 5 minutes). Stir in beans, mustard, tomato sauce, and cheese. Spoon into a shallow 1-quart baking dish. Bake in a 350° oven until cheese is melted (about 25 minutes). Makes 4 servings.

Per serving: 256 calories (62 percent from fat), 10 g protein, 15 g carbohydrates, 18 g total fat (11 g saturated fat), 53 mg cholesterol, 646 mg sodium

Buttered Green Beans & Onions

Contrasting colors and complementary flavors make this combination of green beans and tiny onions a winner.

- 2 pounds green beans, cut into slanting slices; or 3 packages (about 9 oz. *each*) frozen cut green beans

- 2 tablespoons butter or margarine
- 1 tablespoon olive oil or salad oil
- 1 clove garlic, minced or pressed
- ¼ cup minced parsley
- ½ teaspoon salt
  Dash *each* of pepper and ground nutmeg
- 1 jar or can (about 1 lb.) small whole onions, drained

If using fresh beans, cook in boiling water until tender-crisp to bite (about 7 minutes). If using frozen beans, cook according to package directions until tender-crisp to bite. Drain beans, immerse in ice water until cool, and drain again.

Melt butter in oil in a wide frying pan over medium heat. Add garlic, parsley, salt, pepper, and nutmeg. Cook, stirring often, for 3 minutes. Add beans and onions. Cook, stirring occasionally, until heated through. Makes 8 to 10 servings.

Per serving: 78 calories (45 percent from fat), 2 g protein, 9 g carbohydrates, 4 g total fat (2 g saturated fat), 7 mg cholesterol, 341 mg sodium

Western Classic

Broccoli with Pine Nuts & Rice

Golden raisins, pine nuts, and a touch of spice add interest to fresh broccoli and rice.

- ⅓ cup pine nuts or slivered almonds
- 1 tablespoon olive oil or salad oil
- ½ cup long-grain white rice
- ¼ cup golden raisins
- 1½ teaspoons chili powder
- 2 cups chicken broth
  About 1¼ pounds broccoli

Toast pine nuts in a wide frying pan over medium heat, stirring often, until lightly browned (3 to 5 minutes). Remove from pan and set aside.

Add oil, rice, raisins, and chili powder to pan. Cook, stirring, until rice is opaque (about 3 minutes). Add broth and stir until blended. Bring to a boil over high heat; then reduce heat, cover, and simmer until rice is barely tender to bite (about 15 minutes). Meanwhile, trim and discard ends of broccoli stalks. Cut florets from stalks; peel stalks and cut crosswise into thin slices. Set aside.

After rice has cooked for 15 minutes, arrange broccoli florets and stalks on top of rice. Cover and continue to cook until broccoli is tender-crisp to bite (about 10 more minutes). Gently stir broccoli into rice mixture; spoon onto a platter and sprinkle with pine nuts. Makes 4 servings.

Per serving: 243 calories (37 percent from fat), 9 g protein, 33 g carbohydrates, 11 g total fat (1 g saturated fat), 0 mg cholesterol, 529 mg sodium

Diced Potatoes in Soy Sauce

Just three ingredients—cubed potatoes, a little butter, and 2 tablespoons of soy sauce—go into this easy accompaniment. Try it with Oven-simmered Beef Brisket or Flank Steak with Mustard-Caper Sauce (both on page 55) for a new twist on meat and potatoes.

3 tablespoons butter or margarine

1½ pounds thin-skinned potatoes, scrubbed and cut into ½-inch cubes

2 tablespoons soy sauce

Place butter in a 9- by 13-inch or 10- by 15-inch rimmed baking pan; set pan in a 450° oven until butter is melted.

Add potatoes to melted butter and stir to coat. Bake, stirring occasionally, until potatoes are tender when pierced (about 20 minutes). Add soy sauce and stir to coat potatoes. Continue to bake until potatoes look dry (about 10 more minutes). Makes 4 servings.

Per serving: 219 calories (36 percent from fat), 4 g protein, 31 g carbohydrates, 9 g total fat (5 g saturated fat), 23 mg cholesterol, 615 mg sodium

PILGRIM JOE'S
Pecan-topped Sweet Potatoes

Delicately sweet and loaded with butter, this fluffy sweet potato dish has been a Thanksgiving tradition for years.

2½ to 3 pounds sweet potatoes or yams, scrubbed

2 eggs

¾ cup firmly packed brown sugar

½ cup (¼ lb.) butter or margarine, melted

1 teaspoon *each* salt and ground cinnamon
    About ½ cup orange juice

1 cup pecan halves

Cook sweet potatoes in boiling water until tender throughout when pierced (about 30 minutes). Drain and let cool briefly; then peel and place in a large bowl. Using an electric mixer or a potato masher, beat potatoes until almost smooth. Add eggs, ¼ cup of the sugar, ¼ cup of the butter, salt, cinnamon, and ½ cup of the orange juice. Continue to beat until moist and fluffy, adding more orange juice if needed.

Spread mixture in a shallow 1½- to 2-quart baking dish. Top with pecans, sprinkle with remaining ½ cup sugar, and drizzle with remaining ¼ cup butter. (At this point, you may cover and refrigerate until next day.)

Bake, uncovered, in a 375° oven until heated through (about 20 minutes; about 40 minutes if refrigerated). Makes 8 to 10 servings.

Per serving: 367 calories (47 percent from fat), 4 g protein, 46 g carbohydrates, 20 g total fat (7 g saturated fat), 75 mg cholesterol, 381 mg sodium

Western Classic
Best-ever Garlicky Potatoes

Potato wedges, onions, and garlic all roast together in this classic side dish. The high oven heat cooks the vegetables to a crisp golden brown outside, but keeps them tender inside.

1 tablespoon olive oil

1 tablespoon butter or margarine

3 large red thin-skinned potatoes, scrubbed and cut into eighths

1 medium-size onion, cut into eighths

3 cloves garlic, peeled and halved
   Salt and pepper

Place oil and butter in a 9- by 13-inch baking pan; set pan in a 475° oven until butter is melted and sizzling.

Add potatoes, onion, and garlic to pan and stir to coat. Bake, stirring occasionally, until potatoes are golden brown and tender when pierced (about 30 minutes). Season vegetables to taste with salt and pepper. Makes 4 servings.

Per serving: 212 calories (28 percent from fat), 4 g protein, 35 g carbohydrates, 7 g total fat (2 g saturated fat), 8 mg cholesterol, 44 mg sodium

Curried New Potatoes & Green Onions

Looking for a new way to dress fried potatoes? Try sautéing them in butter, with green onions, curry, and mustard seeds.

3 pounds small thin-skinned potatoes, scrubbed
   About ½ cup (¼ lb.) butter or margarine

2 teaspoons *each* curry powder and mustard seeds

2 cups sliced green onions
   Salt

Cook potatoes in boiling water until tender throughout when pierced (about 20 minutes). Drain and let cool briefly; then coarsely chop.

Melt ½ cup of the butter in a wide frying pan over high heat. Add potatoes and cook, stirring often, for about 5 minutes; add more butter if needed to prevent sticking. Sprinkle curry powder and mustard seeds over potatoes and stir until blended. Continue to cook, stirring often, until potatoes are lightly browned. Stir in onions and cook, stirring, until onions are warm. Season to taste with salt. Makes 8 to 10 servings.

Per serving: 225 calories (42 percent from fat), 4 g protein, 29 g carbohydrates, 11 g total fat (6 g saturated fat), 28 mg cholesterol, 120 mg sodium

PASTA & GRAINS

Spaghetti, lasagne, risotto—the names may be foreign, but in the West, as elsewhere in America, these dishes have been suppertime standards for years. ● *We include some of the tried-and-true favorites in this chapter, but many of the recipes in these pages are relatively recent. Quite a few date from the 1980s and early '90s, when the availability of more and different pasta and grain varieties attracted the interest of Western cooks—and inspired them to create new versions of classic specialties. Red peppers, chiles, even salmon take on a new role; black beans and tomatoes go into an unusual Mexican-style filling for lasagne. Even simple pilaf becomes a new dish when it's made with oats or accented with dried fruit.*

Scallop & Red Pepper Pasta

By pairing scallops with pasta, you can stretch a pound of this delectable but rather expensive seafood to feed four to six diners. Vary the amount of crushed red pepper to make the sauce as spicy as you like.

1	lemon
12	ounces dry spaghetti
1	pound scallops
¼	cup butter or margarine
¼	cup olive oil
3	large red bell peppers, seeded and cut into thin slivers
2	cloves garlic, minced or pressed
¼	to ½ teaspoon crushed red pepper flakes
¾	cup chicken broth
¼	cup lemon juice
¾	cup finely chopped parsley
	Salt and pepper

Using a zester, cut peel (colored part only) from lemon in fine shreds (or use a vegetable peeler to pare off colored part of peel, then cut peel into fine slivers). Set lemon peel aside. In a large pan, cook pasta in about 3 quarts of boiling salted water until tender to bite (8 to 10 minutes). Drain, rinse with cold water, and drain again; set aside. Rinse scallops and pat dry; if using sea scallops, cut into ¼-inch-thick slices. Set aside.

Melt butter in oil in a wide frying pan over medium-high heat. Add bell peppers, garlic, and red pepper flakes; cook, stirring, for 1 minute. Add broth and lemon juice to pan; bring to a boil. Add scallops, cover, and cook until opaque in center; cut to test (about 3 minutes). Remove from heat. Lift scallops and peppers from pan with a slotted spoon and set aside.

Add pasta to pan juices; lift and mix with 2 forks until pasta is hot.

Pour pasta and sauce into a serving dish. Top with scallops and peppers; then sprinkle with parsley and lemon peel. Season to taste with salt and pepper. Before serving, mix lightly with a serving fork and spoon. Makes 4 to 6 servings.

Per serving: 538 calories (37 percent from fat), 25 g protein, 59 g carbohydrates, 22 g total fat (7 g saturated fat), 55 mg cholesterol, 400 mg sodium

Mostaccioli & Swiss Cheese Casserole

In this savory baked version of macaroni and cheese, mostaccioli—the name means "little mustaches" in Italian—mingle with Swiss cheese, spinach, and slivered ham in a piquant mustard sauce.

8	ounces dry mostaccioli or other dry small tube-shaped pasta, such as penne or ziti
¼	cup butter or margarine
¼	cup all-purpose flour
2	cups milk
¼	teaspoon liquid hot pepper seasoning
1	tablespoon Dijon mustard
3	cups (about 12 oz.) shredded Swiss cheese
½	pound cooked ham, cut into thin, bite-size slivers
1	package (about 10 oz.) frozen leaf spinach, thawed and squeezed dry
	Salt and pepper

In a large pan, cook pasta in about 2½ quarts of boiling salted water until barely tender to bite (10 to 12 minutes); or cook according to package directions. Drain, rinse, and drain again; set aside.

In pan used to cook pasta, melt butter over medium heat. Stir in flour and cook, stirring, for 1 minute (do not brown). Remove from heat and gradually stir in milk. Return to heat and cook, stirring constantly, until sauce

boils and thickens. Add hot pepper seasoning, mustard, and 2 cups of the cheese; stir until cheese is melted.

Remove cheese sauce from heat and add pasta and ham; mix gently. Stir in spinach. Spread in a shallow 2-quart baking dish.

(Continued on next page)

PASTA

Legend has Marco Polo bringing pasta back from China (where records date it back to circa 1000 B.C.) to Italy in the 13th century. While the spaghetti shape may be from China, the ancient Romans enjoyed flat, ribbonlike fettucine noodles as early as the 4th century A.D.

When deciding between fresh and dry pasta, aficionados agree on a few simple differences. Dry pasta is usually denser and chewier than fresh, so it can stand up to thick sauces replete with chunks. Dry varieties take longer to cook—8 to 12 minutes depending on the cut. Soft-textured fresh pasta, by contrast, is a natural match for the more delicate cream sauces and herb-infused oils; it cooks very rapidly, often in a minute or two.

... Mostaccioli

Bake, covered, in a 350° oven for 20 minutes (30 minutes if refrigerated). Uncover, sprinkle with remaining 1 cup cheese, and continue to bake until cheese is melted and casserole is bubbly (about 10 more minutes). Season to taste with salt and pepper. Makes 6 servings.

Per serving: 571 calories (48 percent from fat), 34 g protein, 40 g carbohydrates, 30 g total fat (18 g saturated fat), 107 mg cholesterol, 1,080 mg sodium

Fettuccine Rapido

When long, busy workdays give you less time to cook, quick side dishes and entrées are the rule. In this simple accompaniment for meats, fish, or poultry, a blend of chiles, garlic, parsley, and olive oil lightly coats fresh fettuccine.

- ⅓ **cup olive oil**
- 2 **small dried hot red chiles, *each* broken into 3 pieces**
- 2 **cloves garlic, minced or pressed**
- ½ **teaspoon salt**
- ½ **cup chopped parsley**
- 8 **ounces fresh or dry fettuccine**

Heat oil in a small pan over low heat. Add chiles and cook, stirring occasionally, until they begin to brown. Add garlic and cook, stirring, for 30 seconds. Add salt and parsley; cook, stirring occasionally, for 1 more minute. Remove from heat.

In a large pan, cook pasta in about 2½ quarts of boiling salted water until barely tender to bite (3 to 4 minutes for fresh pasta, about 8 minutes for dry); or cook according to package directions. Drain pasta and transfer to a serving bowl. Pour sauce over pasta and toss gently until lightly coated. Makes 4 servings.

Per serving: 344 calories (51 percent from fat), 8 g protein, 35 g carbohydrates, 20 g total fat (3 g saturated fat), 67 mg cholesterol, 294 mg sodium

Pasta with Shrimp in Tomato Cream

There are a number of tempting uses for oil-packed dried tomatoes. In this recipe, both the intensely flavored tomatoes and the oil go into an easy, vermouth-spiked shrimp sauce.

- ⅓ **cup dried tomatoes packed in oil**
- 1 **clove garlic, minced or pressed**
- 1 **pound large raw shrimp, shelled and deveined**
- ¼ **cup thinly sliced green onions**
- 1½ **tablespoons chopped fresh basil or 1 teaspoon dry basil**
- ¼ **teaspoon white pepper**
- 1 **cup chicken broth**
- ¾ **cup dry vermouth**
- 1 **cup whipping cream**
- 10 **ounces dry linguine**
   Basil sprigs (optional)
   Grated Parmesan cheese

Drain tomatoes, reserving 2 tablespoons of the oil. Pour oil into a wide frying pan. Sliver tomatoes and set aside. Heat oil over medium-high heat. Add garlic and shrimp. Cook, stirring often, until shrimp are just opaque in center; cut to test (4 to 5 minutes). Lift out and set aside.

Add tomatoes, onions, chopped basil, white pepper, broth, vermouth, and cream to pan. Bring to a boil over high heat; boil, stirring occasionally, until reduced to about 1½ cups.

Meanwhile, in a large pan, cook pasta in about 3 quarts of boiling salted water until barely tender to bite (8 to 10 minutes); or cook according to package directions. Drain and divide among 4 dinner plates.

Return cooked shrimp to sauce; stir just until heated through. Spoon sauce equally over pasta. Garnish with basil sprigs, if desired. Offer cheese to add to taste. Makes 4 servings.

Per serving: 703 calories (44 percent from fat), 31 g protein, 62 g carbohydrates, 32 g total fat (13 g saturated fat), 206 mg cholesterol, 662 mg sodium

Fettuccine Alfredo

Lightly browned butter, Parmesan, and plenty of whipping cream add up to a luxurious sauce for fettuccine. Paired with a crisp green salad, the dish makes a satisfying supper.

- 8 **ounces dry fettuccine**
- ¼ **cup butter or margarine**
- 1½ **cups whipping cream**
- 1 **cup (about 4 oz.) grated Parmesan cheese**
   Salt and pepper
   Whole or ground nutmeg

In a large pan, cook pasta in about 2½ quarts of boiling salted water until barely tender to bite (about 8 minutes); or cook according to package directions. Drain.

While pasta is cooking, melt butter in a wide frying pan over high heat; cook until lightly browned. Add ½ cup of the cream and bring to a boil; boil, stirring constantly, until slightly thickened. Reduce heat to medium. Add cooked pasta to sauce and toss gently. Then add ½ cup of the cheese and ½ cup more cream; toss gently. Add ½ cup cheese and ½ cup cream; toss gently again. Season to taste with salt and pepper. Grate nutmeg generously over top. Makes 2 to 4 servings.

Per serving: 945 calories (63 percent from fat), 29 g protein, 59 g carbohydrates, 67 g total fat (41 g saturated fat), 276 mg cholesterol, 916 mg sodium

Tortellini with Broccoli & Gorgonzola

Italian ingredients and Asian cooking techniques come together deliciously in this robust stir-fry. For a complete meal, add a crisp green salad and crusty fresh bread.

- 1 **pound skinless, boneless chicken breasts**
- 3 **tablespoons butter or margarine**
- ¾ **cup walnuts or pecans (halves or large pieces)**
- 5 **cups (about 1 lb.) broccoli florets, cut into bite-size pieces**
  About 1¾ cups chicken broth
- 1 **package (about 12 oz.) frozen tortellini, 12 ounces fresh tortellini, or 1 package (7 or 8 oz.) dry tortellini**
- ½ **cup finely chopped onion**
- 4 **teaspoons cornstarch**
- ½ **cup firmly packed Gorgonzola or other blue-veined cheese, crumbled**
- ½ **teaspoon pepper**
- 1 **tablespoon white wine vinegar**

Rinse chicken breasts, pat dry, and cut crosswise into ¼-inch-thick slices. Set aside.

Melt 1 tablespoon of the butter in a wok or wide frying pan over medium heat. Add walnuts and cook, stirring often, until crisp (about 7 minutes); do not scorch. Pour nuts onto paper towels and let drain.

Wipe pan clean. Melt 1 more tablespoon butter in pan over high heat.

Add chicken. Cook, stirring, until no longer pink in center; cut to test (about 3 minutes). Transfer to a bowl.

To pan, add broccoli and 2 tablespoons of the broth. Cover and cook, stirring occasionally, until broccoli stems are tender when pierced (8 to 10 minutes); add more broth as needed. Lift broccoli from pan with a slotted spoon and add to chicken.

In a large pan, cook tortellini in about 3½ quarts of boiling salted water until barely tender to bite (about 7 minutes for frozen tortellini, 4 to 6 minutes for fresh, 15 to 20 minutes for dry); or cook according to package directions. Drain.

While pasta is cooking, wipe pan clean again. Add remaining 1 tablespoon butter and onion; cook over medium-high heat, stirring often, until onion is soft (about 4 minutes). Sprinkle cornstarch evenly over onion; stir to mix well. Add 1¼ cups of the broth and bring to a boil, stirring constantly.

Reduce heat to low. Crumble in about three-fourths of the cheese; stir until smoothly blended. Add pepper, chicken, broccoli, and tortellini. Stir gently until heated through; cut into pasta to test (about 5 minutes). Stir in vinegar and pour into a serving bowl. Sprinkle with walnuts and remaining cheese. Makes 4 servings.

Per serving: 719 calories (41 percent from fat), 52 g protein, 55 g carbohydrates, 34 g total fat (10 g saturated fat), 148 mg cholesterol, 1,175 mg sodium

Penne with Smoked Salmon

A splash of vodka enhances the flavor of a creamy, tomato-dotted sauce for smoked salmon and pasta tubes. Impressive in appearance and not too filling, the dish makes a wonderful introduction to an elegant dinner.

- 12 **ounces dry penne or other dry small tube-shaped pasta, such as mostaccioli or ziti**
- 2 **tablespoons olive oil**
- 1 **small shallot, thinly sliced**
- 4 **small pear-shaped (Roma-type) tomatoes, peeled, seeded, and chopped**
- ⅔ **cup whipping cream**
  Pinch of ground nutmeg
- 2 **tablespoons chopped fresh dill or ½ teaspoon dry dill weed**
- ⅓ **cup vodka**
- 4 **to 6 ounces sliced smoked salmon or lox, cut into bite-size strips**
  White pepper
  Dill sprigs

In a large pan, cook pasta in about 3 quarts of boiling salted water until barely tender to bite (10 to 12 minutes); or cook according to package directions. Drain.

While pasta is cooking, heat oil in a wide frying pan over medium-low heat. Add shallot and cook, stirring often, until soft but not browned (about 3 minutes). Stir in tomatoes, cover, and simmer for 5 minutes. Add cream, nutmeg, chopped dill, and vodka. Bring to a boil over high heat; boil for 1 minute.

Add pasta to sauce; toss gently to coat. Remove from heat, add salmon, and mix lightly. Season to taste with white pepper and garnish with dill sprigs. Makes 4 servings.

Per serving: 586 calories (37 percent from fat), 19 g protein, 67 g carbohydrates, 22 g total fat (9 g saturated fat), 53 mg cholesterol, 592 mg sodium

Noodles Romanoff

First featured in our "Kitchen Cabinet" in 1956, this noodle casserole is delicious with any simple entrée, from poached fish to grilled chicken.

- **8 ounces dry medium-wide egg noodles, linguine, or fettuccine**
- **1 cup cottage cheese**
- **1 small clove garlic, minced or pressed**
- **1 teaspoon Worcestershire**
- **1 cup sour cream**
- **¼ cup grated onion**
- **¼ teaspoon liquid hot pepper seasoning**
- **½ cup shredded Cheddar cheese**

In a large pan, cook noodles in about 2½ quarts of boiling salted water until barely tender to bite (about 8 minutes); or cook according to package directions. Drain and transfer to a large bowl. Add cottage cheese, garlic, Worcestershire, sour cream, onion, and hot pepper seasoning; stir gently until combined. Pour into a greased shallow 2-quart baking dish and sprinkle with Cheddar cheese. Bake in a 350° oven until heated through (about 25 minutes). Makes 6 to 8 servings.

Per serving: 261 calories (42 percent from fat), 11 g protein, 26 g carbohydrates, 12 g total fat (7 g saturated fat), 58 mg cholesterol, 319 mg sodium

Penne with Broccoli & Ricotta

Mild-flavored ricotta is lower in fat than many other cheeses. Here, it combines with penne and broccoli in a simple entrée that's rich in fiber, vitamins, calcium, and iron.

- **2 tablespoons olive oil**
- **5 green onions, thinly sliced**
- **1 pound broccoli florets, cut into bite-size pieces**
- **¼ cup water**
  Coarsely ground pepper
- **12 ounces dry penne or other dry small tube-shaped pasta, such as mostaccioli or ziti**
- **1½ cups part-skim ricotta cheese**
  Grated Parmesan cheese

Heat oil in a wide frying pan over medium-high heat. Add onions and cook, stirring often, for 1 minute. Add broccoli and cook, stirring often, until bright green (about 3 more minutes). Add ¼ cup water and bring to a boil; then reduce heat, cover, and simmer until broccoli is tender-crisp to bite (about 5 minutes). Remove from heat and season to taste with pepper; keep warm.

In a large pan, cook pasta in about 3 quarts of boiling salted water until barely tender to bite (10 to 12 minutes); or cook according to package directions. Drain, reserving about ¼ cup of the cooking water, and transfer pasta to a large serving bowl. Add broccoli mixture and ricotta cheese to pasta; toss gently until combined. If mixture is too dry, stir in enough of the reserved pasta water to moisten. Offer Parmesan cheese to add to taste. Makes 4 servings.

Per serving: 540 calories (26 percent from fat), 25 g protein, 75 g carbohydrates, 16 g total fat (6 g saturated fat), 29 mg cholesterol, 440 mg sodium

Black Bean Lasagne

Protein-rich black beans replace the meat in a vegetarian lasagne accented with cilantro and garlic.

- **4 pounds pear-shaped (Roma-type) tomatoes, cut into halves lengthwise**
- **1½ tablespoons olive oil or salad oil**
- **2 cloves garlic, minced or pressed**
- **1 cup firmly packed chopped cilantro**
- **10 dry lasagne noodles (about 5 oz. *total*)**
- **3 cans (about 15 oz. *each*) black beans, drained and rinsed**
- **¼ cup chicken broth**
- **1 teaspoon ground cumin**
- **½ teaspoon chili powder**
- **2 tubs (about 15 oz. *each*) part-skim ricotta cheese**
- **4 cups (about 1 lb.) shredded jack cheese**
  Salt

Place tomato halves, cut side up, in a 10- by 15-inch rimmed baking pan (a few tomatoes can rest on top of each other). Sprinkle evenly with oil and garlic. Bake in a 425° oven until well browned on top (about 1 hour). Let cool slightly. Remove and discard skins. Place tomatoes in a colander and press them lightly to drain off watery liquid; then transfer to a blender or food processor, add cilantro, and whirl until smooth. (At this point, you may cover and refrigerate for up to 2 days.)

In a large pan, cook noodles in about 2 quarts of boiling salted water until barely tender to bite (10 to 12 minutes); or cook according to package directions. Drain, rinse with cold water, and drain again.

In a bowl, combine beans, broth, cumin, and chili powder. With a potato masher or the back of a large spoon, coarsely mash beans until liquid is incorporated. In another bowl, stir together ricotta cheese and 2½ cups of the jack cheese.

Arrange 5 of the noodles, slightly overlapping, over bottom of a lightly greased 8- by 12-inch or 9- by 13-inch baking dish. Top with half each of the bean mixture, ricotta mixture, and tomato sauce. Repeat layers, ending with sauce. Sprinkle with remaining 1½ cups jack cheese. (At this point, you may cover and refrigerate until next day.)

Bake, uncovered, in a 375° oven until casserole is bubbly and browned on top (about 40 minutes; 50 to 55 minutes if refrigerated). Let stand for about 5 minutes before serving. Season to taste with salt. Makes 6 to 8 servings.

Per serving: 698 calories (44 percent from fat), 44 g protein, 55 g carbohydrates, 34 g total fat (7 g saturated fat), 94 mg cholesterol, 789 mg sodium

Lasagne Belmonte

Never-fail recipes like this one are family pleasers. For a spicier lasagne, mix half a pound of Italian sausages in with the beef.

3 tablespoons olive oil or salad oil

1 medium-size onion, chopped

1½ pounds lean ground beef

1 clove garlic, minced or pressed

2 cans (about 8 oz. *each*) tomato sauce

1 can (about 6 oz.) tomato paste

½ cup *each* dry red wine and water

1 teaspoon *each* salt and dry oregano

½ teaspoon *each* pepper and sugar

12 ounces dry lasagne noodles

2 cups part-skim ricotta cheese

8 ounces mozzarella cheese, thinly sliced

½ cup grated Parmesan cheese

Heat oil in a wide frying pan over medium heat. Add onion and cook, stirring often, until soft (about 5 minutes). Crumble in beef and add garlic; cook, stirring, until meat is browned. Stir in tomato sauce, tomato paste, wine, and water. Then add salt, oregano, pepper, and sugar; stir until blended. Bring to a boil; then reduce heat, cover, and simmer, stirring occasionally, for about 1½ hours.

Meanwhile, in a large pan, cook noodles in about 3 quarts of boiling salted water until barely tender to bite (10 to 12 minutes); or cook according to package directions. Drain, rinse with cold water, and drain again.

Arrange a third of the noodles over bottom of a lightly greased 9- by 13-inch baking dish (lay one layer of noodles lengthwise in dish, the next layer crosswise; continue in this way as you assemble lasagne). Spread a third of the meat sauce over noodles; top with a third each of the ricotta and mozzarella cheeses. Repeat layers twice, ending with mozzarella cheese. Sprinkle with Parmesan cheese.

Bake in a 350° oven until bubbly and browned on top (about 30 minutes). Let stand for about 5 minutes before serving. Makes 6 to 8 servings.

Per serving: 792 calories (52 percent from fat), 42 g protein, 52 g carbohydrates, 45 g total fat (20 g saturated fat), 139 mg cholesterol, 1,423 mg sodium

Spicy Lasagne

Follow directions for **Lasagne Belmonte,** but reduce ground beef to 1 pound. Along with beef, add ½ pound **Italian sausages,** casings removed and meat chopped. Makes 6 to 8 servings.

Per serving: 818 calories (54 percent from fat), 41 g protein, 52 g carbohydrates, 48 g total fat (21 g saturated fat), 139 mg cholesterol, 1,638 mg sodium

Vegetable Lasagne

Fitness-conscious pasta lovers ask for meatless lasagne. This version, with five different vegetables and three types of cheese, is our favorite.

1 package (about 8 oz.) dry lasagne noodles

4 carrots (about ¾ lb. *total*), cut into ¼-inch-thick slices

3 zucchini (about 1 lb. *total*), cut into ¼-inch-thick slices

2 tablespoons olive oil or salad oil

1 medium-size onion, chopped

½ pound mushrooms, thinly sliced

1 teaspoon *each* dry basil, dry thyme, and dry oregano

1 large jar (about 30 oz.) marinara sauce

2 packages (about 10 oz. *each*) frozen chopped spinach, thawed and squeezed dry

1 cup part-skim ricotta cheese

3 cups (about 12 oz.) shredded mozzarella cheese

¼ cup grated Parmesan cheese

In a large pan, bring 3 quarts water to a boil over high heat. Add noodles and carrots; cook for 6 minutes. Add zucchini; continue to cook until noodles are barely tender to bite (4 to 5 more minutes). Drain, rinse with cold water, and drain again. Set noodles, carrots, and zucchini aside, keeping noodles and vegetables separate.

In pan used to cook noodles, combine oil, onion, mushrooms, basil, thyme, and oregano. Cook over high heat, stirring often, until onion is soft and liquid has evaporated (5 to 8 minutes). Remove from heat and stir in marinara sauce. In a small bowl, mix spinach and ricotta cheese.

Spread a third of the sauce over bottom of a shallow 2½- to 3-quart baking dish. Arrange half the noodles over sauce. Over noodles, evenly layer half each of the carrots, zucchini, spinach mixture, and mozzarella cheese. Repeat layers, ending with sauce. Sprinkle with Parmesan cheese. (At this point, you may cover and refrigerate until next day.)

Place baking dish on a rimmed baking sheet and bake, uncovered, in a 400° oven until lasagne is bubbly and heated through (about 25 minutes). If refrigerated, bake, uncovered, in a 350° oven until bubbly and heated through (about 50 minutes). Let stand for about 5 minutes before serving. Makes 6 to 8 servings.

Per serving: 516 calories (42 percent from fat), 25 g protein, 53 g carbohydrates, 25 g total fat (11 g saturated fat), 58 mg cholesterol, 1,222 mg sodium

Quick Artichoke Pasta Salad

Marinated artichoke hearts add pep to this vegetable-laden macaroni salad. The dish keeps well, making it a good choice for a picnic or buffet.

1 **cup dry salad macaroni or other medium-size pasta**
1 **jar (about 6 oz.) marinated artichoke hearts**
¼ **pound small mushrooms**
1 **cup cherry tomatoes, cut into halves**
1 **cup medium-size pitted ripe olives**
1 **tablespoon chopped parsley**
½ **teaspoon dry basil**
Salt and pepper

In a large pan, cook macaroni in about 1½ quarts of boiling salted water until tender to bite (about 7 minutes); or cook according to package directions. Drain macaroni well, rinse with cold water, and drain again. Transfer to a large bowl.

Drain liquid from artichokes over macaroni. Cut artichokes into halves or thirds. Add artichokes, mushrooms, cherry tomatoes, olives, parsley, and basil to macaroni. Toss gently. Season to taste with salt and pepper. Cover and refrigerate for at least 4 hours or until next day before serving. Makes 6 servings.

Per serving: 132 calories (32 percent from fat), 4 g protein, 19 g carbohydrates, 5 g total fat (0.7 g saturated fat), 0 mg cholesterol, 346 mg sodium

Lemon-Mint Pea & Pastina Salad

This light salad, introduced in 1988, travels well. To take it to a picnic, pack it in a container and bring the lettuce separately.

1 **cup orzo, riso, or other tiny pasta shapes**
1 **package (about 1 lb.) frozen tiny peas, thawed**
1 **cup chopped celery**
½ **cup *each* thinly sliced green onions and chopped fresh mint**
½ **cup salad oil or olive oil**
¼ **cup lemon juice**
2 **teaspoons grated lemon peel**
Salt and pepper
Romaine lettuce leaves, rinsed and crisped
Mint sprigs

In a large pan, cook pasta in about 3 quarts of boiling salted water just until barely tender to bite (about 5 minutes); or cook according to package directions. Drain, rinse with cold water, and drain again.

In a large bowl, combine pasta, peas, celery, onions, and chopped mint. (At this point, you may cover and refrigerate until next day.) In a small bowl, whisk together oil, lemon juice, and lemon peel. Add to pea mixture; stir to mix well. Season to taste with salt and pepper. If made ahead, cover and refrigerate for up to 2 hours.

To serve, line 8 salad plates with lettuce leaves. Top equally with pea mixture; garnish with mint sprigs. Makes 8 servings.

Per serving: 270 calories (47 percent from fat), 7 g protein, 29 g carbohydrates, 14 g total fat (2 g saturated fat), 0 mg cholesterol, 94 mg sodium

Basil & Scallop Pasta Salad

This combination of seafood, broccoli, pasta, and basil is perfect for a light entrée. Use either the smaller bay scallops or larger sea scallops.

8 **ounces dry pasta spirals or shells**
4 **cups (about ¾ lb.) broccoli florets, cut into 1-inch pieces**
1 **pound scallops, cut into ¼-inch-thick slices if large**
¼ **cup *each* lemon juice and white wine vinegar**
½ **cup *each* olive oil and salad oil**
1 **teaspoon *each* dry mustard and sugar**
1 **clove garlic, minced or pressed**
1 **cup finely chopped fresh basil**
Salt and pepper

In a large pan, cook pasta in about 2½ quarts of boiling salted water until tender to bite (about 8 minutes); or cook according to package directions. Drain, rinse with cold water, and drain again.

In a wide frying pan, boil ¼ inch of water over medium-high heat. Add broccoli, cover, and cook until tender-crisp (about 2 minutes). Drain, immerse in ice water until cool, and drain again. Set aside. Add another ¼ inch of water to pan; bring to a boil, then add scallops. Cover and cook until scallops are opaque in center; cut to test (about 3 minutes). Drain.

In a large bowl, combine pasta, broccoli, and scallops. In a small bowl, whisk together lemon juice, vinegar, olive oil, salad oil, mustard, sugar, garlic, and basil. Pour dressing over broccoli mixture; mix gently. Season to taste with salt and pepper. Cover and refrigerate for at least 2 hours or until next day. Makes 4 to 6 servings.

Per serving: 670 calories (60 percent from fat), 24 g protein, 44 g carbohydrates, 45 g total fat (6 g saturated fat), 30 mg cholesterol, 168 mg sodium

Bulgur Mexicana

A California chef shared this vegetarian tostada with us in 1991. Spoon the Mexican-spiced bulgur over warm, soft tortillas; then roll up to eat out of hand like a burrito, or leave them open-faced and use a knife and fork.

2 tablespoons salad oil

1 large onion, chopped

¾ cup bulgur (quick-cooking cracked wheat)

2 cans (about 10 oz. *each*) enchilada sauce

1 can (about 14½ oz.) Mexican-style stewed tomatoes

⅔ cup toasted wheat germ

1 package (about 10 oz.) frozen chopped Swiss chard or spinach, thawed and squeezed dry

2 fresh jalapeño chiles, seeded and finely chopped

½ teaspoon dry oregano

1 small can (about 8 oz.) red kidney beans, drained and rinsed

6 flour tortillas (*each* about 8 inches in diameter)

Cilantro sprigs

Purchased chile salsa

Plain yogurt

Heat oil in a wide frying pan over medium heat. Add onion and bulgur; cook, stirring often, until onion is soft (about 5 minutes). Stir in enchilada sauce, tomatoes, wheat germ, chard, chiles, oregano, and beans. Cover and simmer, stirring often, until all liquid has been absorbed (10 to 15 minutes).

Meanwhile, stack tortillas and wrap in foil. Heat in a 350° oven until warm and soft (about 15 minutes).

Pour bulgur mixture into a serving bowl and garnish with cilantro sprigs. Accompany with warm tortillas; offer salsa and yogurt to add to taste. Makes 6 servings.

Per serving: 364 calories (21 percent from fat), 14 g protein, 61 g carbohydrates, 9 g total fat (1 g saturated fat), 0 mg cholesterol, 1,436 mg sodium

Couscous with Chanterelles & Herbs

Couscous—processed semolina wheat formed into tiny pellets—is often used in North African and Mideastern dishes. In this recipe, the little grains are permeated with the woodsy flavor and aroma of fresh chanterelles. (Look for the trumpet-shaped mushrooms in well-stocked produce markets.)

4 to 5 ounces fresh chanterelles

2 tablespoons olive oil or salad oil

½ cup finely chopped onion

2 teaspoons minced fresh rosemary or 1 teaspoon dry rosemary

1 teaspoon minced fresh thyme or ½ teaspoon dry thyme

1¾ cups chicken broth

1 cup couscous

¼ cup grated Parmesan cheese

If ends of chanterelles are tough or discolored, trim them off. Immerse chanterelles in water and swish vigorously to remove debris; at once lift from water and drain well. Finely chop chanterelles.

In a wide frying pan, combine chanterelles, oil, onion, rosemary, and thyme. Cover and cook over medium-high heat until mushrooms release their liquid (3 to 5 minutes). Uncover and cook, stirring often, until liquid has evaporated and mushrooms are lightly browned (about 10 minutes).

Add broth and bring to a boil. Stir in couscous, then cover tightly and remove from heat. Let stand until liquid has been absorbed (about 5 minutes). With a fork, fluff couscous; then stir in cheese. Makes 6 servings.

Per serving: 190 calories (30 percent from fat), 7 g protein, 26 g carbohydrates, 6 g total fat (1 g saturated fat), 3 mg cholesterol, 354 mg sodium

Oat Pilaf

Pilafs made with steel-cut oats are chunkier and heartier than those using rice. Try this dense-textured dish alongside a hearty main course such as Golden Chicken Cutlets (page 57).

3 tablespoons butter or margarine

1 large onion, thinly sliced

1 cup steel-cut oats or oat groats

1¾ cups beef broth (2¼ cups if using oat groats)

Parsley sprigs

Melt butter in a wide frying pan over medium-high heat. Add onion and cook, stirring often, until soft (about 4 minutes). Add oats and stir for 1 minute. Then pour in broth.

Bring to a boil over high heat; then reduce heat, cover, and simmer, stirring occasionally, until liquid has been absorbed (about 15 minutes for steel-cut oats, about 40 minutes for oat groats). Garnish with parsley sprigs. Makes 4 servings.

Per serving: 276 calories (38 percent from fat), 9 g protein, 35 g carbohydrates, 12 g total fat (6 g saturated fat), 23 mg cholesterol, 452 mg sodium

A staple for half the world's population, rice is a basic food in both Asia and Europe. Italians serve it plumped with broth in creamy risotto; in the Mideast, it's featured in fragrant pilafs.

In feudal Japan, landowners measured wealth and power by the size of their rice harvest—and used the grain as currency to pay samurai for protection and services. In China, where rice is the principal crop, the pearly grain was declared sacred in 2800 B.C. Today, per capita consumption of rice in China remains high—about 1 pound per day.

Rice Pilaf with Fruit & Nuts

- 5 cups chicken broth
- ½ cup (¼ lb.) butter or margarine
- ½ teaspoon sugar
- 2 cups long-grain white rice
  Salt
- 3 tablespoons butter or margarine
- 1 cup whole blanched almonds
- 1 cup raisins or dried currants
- 1 cup pitted dates, cut into quarters
- 1 cup dried apricots, cut into quarters

In a large pan, combine broth, the ½ cup butter, and sugar. Bring to a boil over high heat. Add rice and stir until mixture returns to a boil. Reduce heat, cover, and simmer for 15 minutes. Season to taste with salt. Pour into a 2½-quart baking dish. Cover and bake in a 325° oven until rice is tender to bite (1 to 1¼ hours).

About 10 minutes before rice is done, melt 1 tablespoon butter in a wide frying pan over medium heat. Add almonds and cook, stirring often, until golden brown (3 to 5 minutes). Lift from pan with a slotted spoon and drain on paper towels. Melt remaining 2 tablespoons butter in pan. Add raisins and stir until puffy. Add dates and stir to coat with butter. Then add apricots and stir until heated through. To serve, pour fruits over rice; sprinkle with almonds. Makes 12 servings.

Per serving: 391 calories (39 percent from fat), 7 g protein, 55 g carbohydrates, 18 g total fat (7 g saturated fat), 28 mg cholesterol, 524 mg sodium

Baked Lemon Rice Pilaf

- 2 cups chicken broth
- 1 cup long-grain white rice
- 2 teaspoons grated lemon peel
- 2 tablespoons lemon juice
- ¼ cup sliced green onions
- 1 tablespoon butter or margarine

In a 1½- to 2-quart baking dish, mix broth, rice, lemon peel, lemon juice, onions, and butter. Cover and bake in a 350° oven until rice is tender to bite (about 50 minutes). Makes 6 servings.

Per serving: 141 calories (17 percent from fat), 3 g protein, 26 g carbohydrates, 3 g total fat (1 g saturated fat), 5 mg cholesterol, 352 mg sodium

Wild Rice with Golden Raisins

- 1¾ cups wild rice
- ¼ cup butter or margarine
- ½ cup golden raisins
- 1 large onion, minced
- 1 teaspoon dry thyme
- 6 cups beef or chicken broth
- 2 tablespoons dry sherry (optional)
- 2 to 3 tablespoons thinly sliced green onions

Rinse rice with water, drain, and set aside.

Melt butter in a 3- to 4-quart pan over medium-high heat. Add raisins and stir until puffy. Lift out with a slotted spoon and set aside.

Add minced onion and thyme to pan; cook, stirring often, until onion is lightly browned (about 9 minutes). Stir in broth and bring to a boil. Add rice and return to a boil over high heat; then reduce heat, cover, and simmer until rice is tender to bite (about 1½ hours), stirring occasionally. Add sherry (if desired), cover, and cook for 10 more minutes. Pour rice into a greased 2-quart baking dish. (At this point, you may let rice cool, then cover and refrigerate rice and raisins separately until next day.)

Bake, uncovered, in a 350° oven for 15 minutes. (If refrigerated, bake covered, until heated through—about 1 hour.) Scatter raisins over rice and bake, uncovered, for 10 more minutes. Sprinkle with green onions. Makes 8 servings.

Per serving: 232 calories (26 percent from fat), 8 g protein, 37 g carbohydrates, 7 g total fat (4 g saturated fat), 16 mg cholesterol, 682 mg sodium

Wild Rice Salad

- 1½ cups wild rice
- 3 cups chicken broth
- ⅓ cup salad oil or olive oil
- 2 tablespoons raspberry or wine vinegar
- 2 tablespoons minced shallots or onion
- 2 teaspoons Dijon mustard
- ¼ teaspoon pepper

Rinse rice with water; drain. In a 2- to 3-quart pan, combine rice and broth; bring to a boil over high heat. Reduce heat to low, cover, and simmer, stirring occasionally, until rice is tender to bite and almost all liquid has been absorbed (about 50 minutes). Remove from heat and let cool.

In a small bowl, whisk together oil, vinegar, shallots, mustard, and pepper. Stir into cooled rice. If made ahead, cover and let stand at room temperature for up to 4 hours or refrigerate for up to 2 days. Bring to room temperature before serving. Makes 8 servings.

Per serving: 201 calories (43 percent from fat), 6 g protein, 24 g carbohydrates, 10 g total fat (1 g saturated fat), 0 mg cholesterol, 411 mg sodium

Brown Rice Vegetable Casserole

2½ cups water
2 chicken bouillon cubes
1 cup long-grain brown rice
1 pound broccoli
1 small head cauliflower
2 medium-size crookneck squash or zucchini
¼ cup sliced celery
¼ pound mushrooms, sliced
¼ cup *each* shredded carrot and sliced green onions
½ teaspoon soy sauce
1 can (about 7 oz.) mild green chile salsa
   About 20 cherry tomatoes
3 slices jack cheese (about 1 oz. *each*)
3 slices Cheddar cheese (about 1 oz. *each*)
3 tablespoons salted roasted sunflower seeds

In a 2-quart pan, combine water and bouillon cubes. Bring to a boil over high heat. Add rice; reduce heat, cover, and simmer until rice is tender to bite (about 45 minutes). Remove from heat and uncover.

While rice is cooking, cut florets from broccoli stalks. Reserve stalks for other uses. Break florets into bite-size pieces, leaving about 2 inches of stem. Break cauliflower into bite-size florets.

Cut squash into ½-inch-thick slices. Arrange broccoli, cauliflower, squash, and celery on a rack in a pan over 1 inch of boiling water. Cover and steam until all vegetables are tender-crisp to bite (8 to 10 minutes). Add mushrooms, cover, and steam for 2 more minutes. Remove vegetables from heat.

Add carrot, onions, and soy sauce to rice; stir gently until combined. Spread rice mixture evenly in a greased shallow 2-quart baking dish. Spoon salsa evenly over rice and top with steamed vegetables and cherry tomatoes. Cut each slice of cheese in half; then cover casserole with alternate slices of jack and Cheddar cheese, overlapping edges slightly. (At this point, you may cover and refrigerate until next day.)

Bake, uncovered, in a 350° oven until heated through (15 to 20 minutes; 25 to 30 minutes if refrigerated). Sprinkle with sunflower seeds. Makes 6 servings.

Per serving: 307 calories (35 percent from fat), 14 g protein, 37 g carbohydrates, 12 g total fat (3 g saturated fat), 27 mg cholesterol, 832 mg sodium

Vegetable Risotto

2 tablespoons olive oil
1 large red bell pepper, seeded and diced
2 medium-size zucchini, diced
¼ cup butter or margarine

1 large onion, chopped
1 clove garlic, minced or pressed
1½ cups short-grain white rice
4 to 4⅓ cups chicken broth
1 package (about 9 oz.) frozen artichoke hearts, thawed
2 cups diced cooked turkey (optional)
1 cup (about 4 oz.) grated Parmesan cheese
   Salt and pepper

Heat oil in a wide frying pan or large pan over medium-high heat. Add bell pepper and zucchini; cook, stirring constantly, until vegetables are tender-crisp to bite (about 5 minutes). Lift out vegetables and set aside.

Reduce heat to medium and add butter, onion, and garlic to pan; cook, stirring often, until onion is soft and golden (about 7 minutes). Add rice and cook, stirring often, until it is opaque and looks milky (about 10 minutes). Stir in 4 cups of the broth; continue to cook, stirring occasionally, until mixture comes to a boil. Reduce heat slightly and boil gently, stirring occasionally, for 10 minutes.

Stir in artichoke hearts, turkey (if desired), bell pepper, and zucchini. Reduce heat to low and continue to cook, stirring often, until rice is tender to bite and almost all liquid has been absorbed (10 to 15 more minutes); if the liquid evaporates before rice is cooked, add a little more broth.

Remove from heat and stir in about ¼ cup of the cheese. Season to taste with salt and pepper. Spoon into a serving dish and sprinkle with about ¼ cup more cheese. Offer remaining cheese to add to taste. Makes 4 servings.

Per serving: 653 calories (40 percent from fat), 23 g protein, 76 g carbohydrates, 29 g total fat (14 g saturated fat), 53 mg cholesterol, 1,709 mg sodium

·

At Sunset, we've always designed our fish and shellfish recipes with the Western cook in mind. In years past, that meant a focus on local varieties—salmon, river trout, and Dungeness crab—in addition to a few long-time classics such as halibut, sole, and shrimp. Today, however, we've expanded our repertoire to reflect the growing number of seafood choices in modern markets. We now offer readers ideas for serving orange roughy, fresh tuna, shark, swordfish, and other once lesser-known types. • *In this chapter, you'll find both traditional favorites and more innovative selections: creamy sauces and quiches from past decades meet the lighter recipes popularized in the '80s and early '90s. Cooking methods vary, too, from familiar pan-frying and oven-baking to steaming, stir-frying, and smoking in a covered barbecue. (For more information on fish-cooking techniques, see pages 48–49.)*

Fish Fillets with Sherry-Mushroom Sauce

Any white fish works well in this recipe, but sea bass, lingcod, and rockfish are particularly good. If you enjoy spicier flavors, try adding a dash of red pepper flakes to the sauce.

1½ **pounds white-fleshed fish fillets (*each* about ¾ inch thick), such as sea bass, lingcod, or rockfish**

2 **tablespoons olive oil, butter, or margarine**

¼ **pound mushrooms, thinly sliced**

1 **teaspoon cornstarch**

⅓ **cup water**

¼ **cup dry sherry**

1 **tablespoon soy sauce**

2 **cloves garlic, minced or pressed**

2 **teaspoons minced fresh ginger**

½ **cup sliced green onions**

Rinse fish, pat dry, and set aside.

Heat 1½ tablespoons of the oil in a wide frying pan over medium heat. Add mushrooms and cook, stirring often, until lightly browned (about 8 minutes); lift out with a slotted spoon and set aside.

Heat remaining 1½ teaspoons oil in pan over medium-high heat. Add fish, a few pieces at a time (do not crowd pan). Cover and cook, turning once, until just opaque but still moist in thickest part; cut to test (about 8 minutes). Transfer fish to a platter and keep warm.

In a small bowl, stir together cornstarch, water, sherry, soy sauce, garlic, and ginger. Pour cornstarch mixture into pan and stir to scrape browned bits free. Stir in mushrooms; bring to a boil, stirring. Stir in onions and pour sauce over fish. Makes 4 servings.

Per serving: 267 calories (38 percent from fat), 33 g protein, 6 g carbohydrates, 10 g total fat (2 g saturated fat), 70 mg cholesterol, 378 mg sodium

Grilled Fish Steaks with Mustard Sauce

Fish cooked over charcoal acquires a mellow smokiness that's enhanced by robust toppings like the mustard sauce we suggest here. Firm fish steaks—swordfish, halibut, sturgeon, and salmon—are all good choices.

1½ **to 2 pounds firm-textured fish steaks (*each* about 1 inch thick)**
   Olive oil or salad oil

¼ **cup *each* dry white wine and whipping cream**

1 **tablespoon Dijon mustard**

2 **tablespoons butter or margarine**
   Salt and pepper
   Chopped parsley

Rinse fish, pat dry, and brush lightly with oil. Place on a well-greased grill 4 to 6 inches above a solid bed of hot coals. Cook, turning once, until fish is just opaque but still moist in thickest part; cut to test (about 10 minutes). Transfer to a platter and keep warm.

In a wide frying pan, bring wine, cream, and mustard to a boil over high heat; boil, stirring occasionally, until reduced to ¼ cup. Remove from heat and whisk in butter; continue to whisk until sauce is thickened. Season sauce to taste with salt and pepper, spoon over fish, and sprinkle with parsley. Makes 4 to 6 servings.

Per serving: 289 calories (56 percent from fat), 30 g protein, 0.8 g carbohydrates, 17 g total fat (7 g saturated fat), 91 mg cholesterol, 249 mg sodium

Broiled Swordfish with Tomato-Olive Confetti

Today, cooks like recipes that focus on flavor and freshness. This delicious dish is a case in point: a bed of watercress sprigs is topped with hot broiled swordfish steaks and a bright tomato-olive salsa. Heat from the cooked fish wilts the cress and warms the tomatoes, intensifying all the flavors.

   Tomato-Olive Confetti (recipe follows)

1½ **pounds swordfish steaks (*each* about 1 inch thick)**

   About 1 tablespoon olive oil or salad oil

3 **cups lightly packed watercress sprigs, rinsed and crisped**

   Lime wedges (optional)

Prepare Tomato-Olive Confetti and set aside.

Rinse fish, pat dry, and cut into 4 equal pieces. Place fish on an oiled rack in a 12- by 14-inch broiler pan; brush fish with oil. Broil fish about 5 inches below heat for 5 minutes. Turn fish over, brush with oil again, and continue to broil until just opaque but still moist in thickest part; cut to test (5 to 6 more minutes).

Divide watercress sprigs equally among 4 dinner plates and place a piece of hot swordfish on each. Spoon Tomato-Olive Confetti evenly over fish. Serve with lime wedges, if desired. Makes 4 servings.

Tomato-Olive Confetti. In a small bowl, stir together 1 medium-size **tomato,** seeded and finely chopped; ½ cup sliced **pimento-stuffed green olives;** 2 tablespoons drained **capers;** 3 tablespoons *each* sliced **green onions** and **lime juice;** and 3 tablespoons **olive oil** or salad oil.

Per serving: 337 calories (59 percent from fat), 31 g protein, 3 g carbohydrates, 22 g total fat (4 g saturated fat), 59 mg cholesterol, 672 mg sodium

Salmon with Chive & Herb Sauce

In this recipe, thick salmon steaks poach in herb-seasoned chicken broth; when the fish is done, you use the broth as the base for a delicate sauce.

- 4 **salmon steaks (about 1½ lbs. total),** *each* **about 1 inch thick**
- 1 **cup chicken broth**
- 2 **teaspoons** *each* **minced fresh tarragon and fresh thyme; or ½ teaspoon** *each* **dry tarragon and dry thyme**
- 1 **clove garlic, minced or pressed**
- 1 **teaspoon cornstarch blended with 2 tablespoons cold water**
- 3 **tablespoons snipped chives**
  Salt and pepper
  Lemon wedges

Rinse fish, pat dry, and set aside. In a wide frying pan, combine broth, tarragon, and thyme. Bring to a boil over high heat; gently lay fish in pan. Reduce heat, cover, and simmer until fish is just opaque but still moist in thickest part; cut to test (10 to 15 minutes). Lift fish to a platter; keep warm.

Add garlic to cooking liquid. Bring to a boil over high heat; boil, stirring occasionally, until reduced to ½ cup. Stir in cornstarch mixture; return to a boil, stirring. Stir in chives, then pour sauce over fish. Season to taste with salt and pepper. Serve with lemon wedges. Makes 4 servings.

Per serving: 225 calories (41 percent from fat), 31 g protein, 1 g carbohydrates, 10 g total fat (1 g saturated fat), 82 mg cholesterol, 313 mg sodium

Salmon Quiche

Because it starts with canned salmon and a purchased pastry shell, this creamy quiche is a snap to prepare.

- 3 **eggs**
- 1¼ **cups half-and-half**
- 2 **tablespoons minced parsley**
- ¼ **teaspoon** *each* **salt and onion powder**
- 1 **can (about 15½ oz.) salmon**
- ¾ **cup shredded mild Cheddar cheese**
  Purchased 9-inch pie shell
- ½ **cup sliced ripe olives**

In a medium-size bowl, beat eggs until blended. Beat in half-and-half, parsley, salt, and onion powder. Set aside. Drain salmon and separate into bite-size chunks. Lightly mix salmon and half the cheese; spoon into pastry shell. Scatter olives and remaining cheese over top. Pour in egg mixture. Bake in a 425° oven for 10 minutes; reduce oven temperature to 350° and continue to bake until filling is set but still moist on top (about 25 more minutes). Let stand for a few minutes before serving. Makes 6 to 8 servings.

Per serving: 350 calories (61 percent from fat), 20 g protein, 14 g carbohydrates, 24 g total fat (9 g saturated fat), 140 mg cholesterol, 693 mg sodium

Canadian Salmon Pie

Shredded potato in the filling makes this salmon pie even heartier. Decorate with pastry cutouts.

- **Tender Pastry (recipe follows)**
- 1 **can (about 15½ oz.) salmon**
- 2 **tablespoons butter or margarine**
- 1 **medium-size onion, chopped**
- 1 **medium-size russet potato, cooked, peeled, and shredded**
- 3 **tablespoons milk**
- 1½ **tablespoons minced fresh dill or ½ teaspoon dry dill weed**
- ¼ **teaspoon freshly ground pepper**
- 1 **teaspoon milk**

Prepare Tender Pastry; refrigerate. Drain salmon and separate into large chunks; set aside.

Melt butter in a medium-size frying pan over medium-high heat. Add onion and cook, stirring often, until soft and golden (about 6 minutes). Remove from heat; gently stir in potato, the 3 tablespoons milk, dill, pepper, and salmon (keep chunks large).

On a floured board, roll out half the pastry to an 11-inch round. Fit into a 9-inch pie pan. Fill with salmon mixture. Roll out remaining pastry to a 10-inch round. Cover pie with pastry; trim and flute edges. If desired, roll out pastry scraps and cut into decorative shapes; place cutouts on top of pie. Cut a few small slashes in top of pie. Gently brush pie with the 1 teaspoon milk.

Bake pie on lowest rack of a 425° oven until pastry is golden brown (30 to 35 minutes). If made ahead, let cool; then cover and refrigerate until next day. To reheat pie, place it in a 350° oven and heat, uncovered, until filling is hot in center (25 to 35 minutes). Makes 8 servings.

Tender Pastry. In a large bowl, mix 2 cups **all-purpose flour,** ¼ teaspoon **salt,** and 1 teaspoon **sugar.** Using a pastry blender or 2 knives, cut in ½ cup **solid vegetable shortening** and 3 tablespoons **butter** or margarine until mixture resembles coarse crumbs. Stir in 1 **egg** (lightly beaten), ½ teaspoon **distilled white vinegar,** and 1½ tablespoons **cold water** until pastry holds together.

Shape pastry into a ball, then divide in half; wrap each half in plastic wrap and refrigerate for at least 1 hour or up to 3 days.

Per serving: 394 calories (54 percent from fat), 15 g protein, 30 g carbohydrates, 24 g total fat (9 g saturated fat), 65 mg cholesterol, 377 mg sodium

Sole Florentine

Spinach, which is what makes a dish "Florentine," is topped with rolled and poached sole fillets cloaked in a well-seasoned cream sauce.

- 4 **small sole fillets (¾ to 1 lb.** ***total*****)**
- 1 **bottle (about 8 oz.) clam juice**
- 1 **package (about 10 oz.) frozen chopped spinach, thawed and squeezed dry**
- ¼ **cup grated Parmesan cheese**
- 2 **tablespoons butter or margarine**
- 2 **tablespoons all-purpose flour**
- ⅔ **cup milk**
- ⅛ **teaspoon ground nutmeg**
- ¼ **teaspoon dry mustard**
- 1 **tablespoon** *each* **lemon juice and instant minced onion**
   Chopped parsley

Rinse fish and pat dry. Loosely roll each fillet, beginning at one end; secure each roll with a wooden pick or skewer. In a medium-size pan, bring clam juice to a boil. Set fish in pan. Reduce heat, cover, and simmer until fish is opaque but still moist in thickest part; cut to test (about 2 minutes). Lift fish from pan and drain on paper towels. Bring clam juice to a boil; boil until reduced to about ½ cup. Pour into a cup and set aside.

Spread spinach evenly over bottom of a shallow 1-quart baking dish or 2 individual casseroles. Sprinkle with 1 tablespoon of the cheese. Remove picks from fish and arrange fish on spinach.

In pan used to cook fish, melt butter over medium-low heat. Stir in flour and cook, stirring, for 1 minute (do not brown). Remove from heat and gradually stir in milk and reduced clam juice. Then return to heat and cook, stirring constantly, until sauce boils and thickens. Stir in nutmeg, mustard, lemon juice, and onion. Spoon sauce over fish and

spinach. Sprinkle with remaining 3 tablespoons cheese.

Bake in a 425° oven until bubbly and lightly browned (10 to 15 minutes). Sprinkle with parsley. Makes 2 servings.

Per serving: 442 calories (41 percent from fat), 48 g protein, 18 g carbohydrates, 20 g total fat (11 g saturated fat), 141 mg cholesterol, 861 mg sodium

TRADER MING'S
Grilled Tuna with Teriyaki Fruit Sauce

For tuna with tropical flair, top fillets or steaks with an exotic soy-ginger sauce and sliced fresh papaya.

- ¼ **cup** *each* **soy sauce and sugar**
- ⅓ **cup sake or dry sherry**
- 3 **quarter-size slices fresh ginger or ¼ teaspoon ground ginger**
- 1 **pound tuna fillets or steaks (***each*** ¾ to 1 inch thick), cut into 4 equal pieces**
   Olive oil or salad oil
- 1 **papaya, peeled, seeded, and cut into 12 slices**
- 2 **teaspoons finely chopped candied or crystallized ginger**
- 1 **green bell pepper, seeded and cut into long, thin slivers**

In a 2-quart pan, combine soy sauce, sugar, sake, and fresh ginger. Bring to a boil over high heat, stirring until sugar is dissolved; then boil until reduced to ⅓ cup. Discard ginger slices and keep sauce warm.

Rinse fish, pat dry, and brush lightly with oil. Place fish on a grill

about 6 inches above a solid bed of hot coals. Cook, turning once, just until browned on outside but still pale pink in center; cut to test (3 to 4 minutes).

To serve, place each piece of fish on a dinner plate. Arrange 3 papaya slices atop each piece of fish; then top each serving equally with soy-ginger sauce and candied ginger. Garnish with bell pepper. Makes 4 servings.

Per serving: 336 calories (34 percent from fat), 28 g protein, 28 g carbohydrates, 12 g total fat (2 g saturated fat), 43 mg cholesterol, 1,079 mg sodium

---

FISH & SHELLFISH
•

At Trader Joe's, we think the best way to insure that the fish you buy is *really* fresh is to buy fish which has been frozen immediately after catching and processing. Our fish is never thawed until you decide to cook it.

Trader Joe's seafood is prepared without sulfites or sodium tripolyphosphates, chemicals commonly used in the seafood industry. These chemicals "plump" up the seafood before freezing by forcing them to absorb and retain more water. Treated fish and shellfish look beautiful when thawed and cooked; however, treated seafood shrinks measurably as the water evaporates in cooking.

To cook any fish perfectly, you'll need to master a few basic techniques—and then learn to match the method to the density, flavor, and fat content of the fish. Rich, firm-textured types take well to grilling and pan-frying, while lighter, soft-fleshed varieties are better suited to gentler procedures such as steaming and poaching.

Whatever technique you use, it's crucial that you know how to test for doneness. Seafood cooks quickly and, as a result, is easily overcooked, losing both moisture and flavor. Fish is done when the flesh has just turned from translucent to opaque, but still looks moist; to check, make a small cut in the center of the thickest part. Don't worry if the fish appears slightly undercooked when it's removed from the pan or oven, since it will continue to cook a bit longer from retained heat.

The recipes in this chapter employ a variety of cooking methods, among them grilling, broiling, steaming, and stir-frying. The techniques described on these two pages are special favorites as well—we've found them to be particularly versatile.

Oven-browning

Oven-browned fish is crisp on the outside, juicy inside. And since timing is less critical when you oven-cook, there's less chance of overcooking.

Medium-dense, flaky-fleshed fish are best for oven-browning. In this recipe, we use an easy crumb coating to give steaks, fillets, or small whole fish a crusty finish.

1 to 1½ pounds fish steaks or fillets (*each* ½ to 1 inch thick); or 4 cleaned small whole fish such as trout

Cheese-Crumb Coating (recipe follows)
3 tablespoons butter or margarine, melted

Rinse fish; pat dry. Prepare Cheese-Crumb Coating.

Pour butter into a shallow dish. Coat fish in butter and let excess drip off; then coat thickly in Cheese-Crumb Coating. Place fish at least 1 inch apart in a foil-lined shallow baking pan.

Bake in a 425° oven until fish is just opaque but still moist in thickest part; cut to test (10 to 20 minutes). Makes 4 servings.

Cheese-Crumb Coating. Crumble 1 slice **firm-textured white bread** into a blender or food processor and whirl until soft crumbs form. In a shallow dish, mix crumbs with 1½ teaspoons grated **Parmesan cheese**, ¼ teaspoon **dry thyme**, and ½ teaspoon **paprika**.

Per serving: 234 calories (47 percent from fat), 27 g protein, 3 g carbohydrates, 12 g total fat (6 g saturated fat), 82 mg cholesterol, 227 mg sodium

Pan-frying

Pan-frying is a great way to cook almost any fillet, steak, or small whole fish.

For even browning, make sure the fish is dry before cooking, and select a pan that heats evenly. A light dusting of flour or a coating of crumbs or cornmeal also helps to ensure uniform browning, especially if you're using thin fillets that cook very quickly. Most thick, firm-fleshed fish, on the other hand, brown well without a coating—and may even overbrown if coated.

1 to 2 pounds fish steaks, fillets, or cleaned small whole fish
Coating (optional; choices and recipes follow)
½ to 2 tablespoons salad oil
½ to 2 tablespoons butter or margarine
Browned Butter Sauce (optional; recipe follows)
Salt and pepper

Rinse fish, pat dry, and cut into serving-size pieces. If desired, prepare coating; working with one piece of fish at a time, coat fish as directed.

Heat 1½ teaspoons each of the oil and butter in a wide frying pan over medium heat. Add fish, a few pieces at a time (do not crowd pan). Cook, turning as needed, until browned on outside and just opaque but still moist in thickest part; cut to test. Allow 2 to 4 minutes for fish less than ½ inch thick; 4 to 8 minutes for fish ½ to ¾ inch thick; and 10 to 15 minutes for fish 1 to 1½ inches thick. Add more oil and butter to pan as needed to prevent sticking. If using Browned Butter Sauce, transfer fish to a platter and keep warm while preparing sauce.

Season fish to taste with salt and pepper; if using sauce, pour sauce over fish. Makes 4 to 6 servings.

Coating. Choose one of the following.

Flour coating. Coat fish in ½ cup **all-purpose flour** and shake off excess.

Light crumb coating. Pour ½ cup **milk** into a shallow dish. In another shallow dish, place ½ cup finely crushed **seasoned croutons** or cracker crumbs; or mix ¼ cup *each* all-purpose flour and yellow cornmeal. Coat fish in milk and let excess drip off; then coat in crumbs and shake off excess.

Heavy crumb coating. In a shallow dish, place ½ cup **all-purpose flour**. In a second shallow dish, beat 2 **eggs** with 2 tablespoons **milk**. In a third shallow dish, place 1 cup **crumbs** (choose from finely crushed seasoned croutons, cornmeal, fine dry bread crumbs, cracker crumbs, wheat germ, or a mixture of ⅓ cup fine dry bread crumbs and ⅔ cup finely ground almonds or walnuts). Coat fish in flour and shake off excess; then coat in egg mixture and let excess drip off. Finally, coat in crumbs and shake off excess. Arrange fish, slightly apart, on a baking sheet and refrigerate for 15 to 30 minutes before cooking.

Browned Butter Sauce. Place ¼ cup **butter** or margarine in a small frying pan. Heat over medium-high heat until butter foams and begins to brown. Remove from heat and stir in 2 tablespoons **lemon juice** and, if desired, 1 tablespoon finely chopped **parsley.**

Per serving without coating or sauce: 154 calories (31 percent from fat), 26 g protein, 0 g carbohydrates, 5 g total fat (0.8 g saturated fat), 65 mg cholesterol, 110 mg sodium

Pan-poaching

Any fish can be pan-poached with excellent results. Even thin fillets, which tend to fall apart quite easily, are well suited to this gentle cooking method. In this recipe, we steam fillets or steaks in a small amount of seasoned liquid; when the fish is done, you can reduce the liquid to make a light sauce.

- **1** to 2 pounds fish fillets or steaks
- **1½** tablespoons butter or margarine
- **3** shallots or 3 green onions, finely chopped or sliced
- **1** clove garlic, minced or pressed
- **½** cup chicken broth; or ¼ cup *each* chicken broth and dry white wine

Rinse fish, pat dry, and set aside.

Melt butter in a wide frying pan over medium heat. Add shallots and

garlic; cook, stirring often, until soft (about 3 minutes). Add broth and bring to a boil. Arrange fish in a single layer in pan. Then reduce heat, cover, and simmer until fish is just opaque but still moist in thickest part; cut to test (3 to 4 minutes for fish ¼ to ⅓ inch thick; 4 to 6 minutes for fish ½ to ¾ inch thick).

With a wide spatula, lift out fish and arrange on a platter; keep warm. Bring pan juices to a boil; then boil until slightly thickened. Spoon sauce over fish. Makes 4 to 6 servings.

Per serving: 162 calories (30 percent from fat), 26 g protein, 1 g carbohydrates, 5 g total fat (3 g saturated fat), 75 mg cholesterol, 245 mg sodium

Cooking in Parchment

When wrapped and baked in parchment, fish steams in its own juices. In addition to sealing in moisture and flavor, the parchment packets make a lasting and elegant impression when brought to the table. Cut through the paper yourself; or let your guests slice the packages open, releasing the tempting aroma of deliciously seasoned seafood.

Despite its impressive looks, parchment-wrapped fish is easy to prepare. It's convenient, too—the packets can be assembled and stored in the refrigerator hours before you plan to cook. The recipe below is easily adjusted to suit your tastes; you might add your choice of cut-up vegetables or replace the dill and tangerine peel with a selection of fresh herbs, for example. (Since the packets bake for only 7 to 10 minutes, any vegetables you include should be parboiled.)

Look for parchment in well-stocked supermarkets, specialty food shops, or cookware stores.

- **3** tablespoons *each* olive oil, white wine vinegar, and thinly sliced green onions
- **1** teaspoon chopped fresh dill or ½ teaspoon dry dill weed
- **1** teaspoon shredded tangerine or orange peel
- **1½** pounds fish fillets, *each* about 1 inch thick (choose fish with medium-dense, flaky flesh)
- **3** tablespoons butter or margarine, melted
  Salt and pepper

In a small bowl, stir together oil, vinegar, onions, dill, and tangerine peel; set aside. Rinse fish, pat dry, and cut into 4 equal pieces.

Cut 4 parchment paper circles, each about 4 times the size of each piece of fish. Brush the center of one half of each circle with about 2 teaspoons of the butter. Set one piece of fish on buttered area of each paper; drizzle with a fourth of the oil mixture, then sprinkle with salt and pepper. To seal each packet, fold free half of parchment circle over fish, forming a semicircle. Beginning at one end, fold about ½ inch of the curved edge closed; continue sealing, making small folds along edge, until entire curve is sealed. (At this point, you may cover and refrigerate packets until next day.)

Place packets slightly apart, folded ends up, on baking sheets. Bake in a 500° oven until fish is just opaque but still moist in thickest part; cut a tiny slit through parchment into fish to test (7 to 10 minutes).

Immediately transfer packets to dinner plates. To serve, cut packets open with a sharp knife or scissors just enough to expose contents without letting juices run out. Makes 4 servings.

Per serving: 335 calories (61 percent from fat), 32 g protein, 0.9 g carbohydrates, 22 g total fat (8 g saturated fat), 93 mg cholesterol, 205 mg sodium

Orange Roughy Maître d'Hôtel

Thanks to its mild, unfishy flavor and firm, tender white flesh, orange roughy is a *Sunset* favorite. Simple enhancements like this one—a tart sauce of butter, lemon, and dill—are best for the delicate-tasting fillets.

⅓   **cup butter or margarine**

¼   **cup *each* lemon juice, chopped parsley, and snipped chives**

2   **teaspoons chopped fresh dill**

¼   **teaspoon ground red pepper (cayenne)**

2   **pounds orange roughy fillets (*each* ½ to ¾ inch thick)**
    Salt

Melt butter in a small pan over medium heat. Stir in lemon juice, parsley, chives, dill, and red pepper; set aside.

Rinse fish, pat dry, and arrange in a single layer, overlapping slightly if necessary, in a 12- by 15-inch baking pan. Pour butter mixture over fish.

Bake in a 400° oven until fish is just opaque but still moist in thickest part; cut to test (8 to 10 minutes). Transfer fish to a serving dish; keep warm. Bring juices in baking pan to a boil over high heat; boil, stirring occasionally, until reduced to about ½ cup. Drain any accumulated juices from fish into sauce; stir sauce and pour over fish. Season to taste with salt. Makes 6 servings.

Per serving: 284 calories (67 percent from fat), 22 g protein, 1 g carbohydrates, 21 g total fat (6 g saturated fat), 58 mg cholesterol, 202 mg sodium

Salmon Fillet with Mustard Glaze

A mustard glaze, lightly sweetened with honey, nicely complements rich-flavored broiled salmon.

1   **boned salmon fillet with skin (1½ to 2 lbs.)**

2   **tablespoons Dijon mustard**

1   **tablespoon *each* olive oil and honey**

¼   **teaspoon grated lemon peel**

1   **tablespoon lemon juice**
    Salt and pepper
    Parsley sprigs
    Lemon wedges

Set a sheet of heavy-duty foil in a 10- by 15-inch rimmed baking pan. Rinse fish and pat dry; then place, skin side down, on foil in pan. With scissors, cut through foil around fish; discard foil trimmings. In a small bowl, stir together mustard, oil, honey, lemon peel, and lemon juice. Brush fish with all of the mustard mixture.

Broil fish about 5 inches below heat until just opaque but still moist in thickest part; cut to test (9 to 12 minutes). Supporting fish with foil, transfer to a platter. Season to taste with salt and pepper. Garnish with parsley sprigs and serve with lemon wedges. Makes 4 to 6 servings.

Per serving: 270 calories (45 percent from fat), 32 g protein, 4 g carbohydrates, 13 g total fat (2 g saturated fat), 87 mg cholesterol, 251 mg sodium

Grilled Soy-Lemon Halibut

True halibut, including both Pacific and Atlantic varieties, is a firm-fleshed fish well suited to grilling. For a light entrée, soak thick steaks in a lemony teriyaki marinade, then cook quickly in a covered barbecue.

2   **pounds halibut, shark, or swordfish steaks (*each* ¾ to 1 inch thick)**

2   **tablespoons butter or margarine, melted**

3   **tablespoons soy sauce**

2   **tablespoons lemon juice**

1   **tablespoon *each* sugar and Worcestershire**

1   **tablespoon minced fresh ginger or ¾ teaspoon ground ginger**

1   **clove garlic, minced or pressed**

⅛   **teaspoon pepper**
    Lemon wedges

Rinse fish and pat dry; cut into serving-size pieces, if necessary.

In a shallow dish, stir together butter, soy sauce, lemon juice, sugar, Worcestershire, ginger, garlic, and pepper. Add fish and turn to coat. Cover and refrigerate for 1 to 2 hours, turning occasionally.

Place fish on a lightly greased grill 4 to 6 inches above a solid bed of hot coals. Cover barbecue and adjust vents as needed to maintain an even heat. Cook, turning once, until fish is just opaque but still moist in thickest part; cut to test (8 to 10 minutes). Serve with lemon wedges. Makes 6 servings.

Per serving: 187 calories (33 percent from fat), 26 g protein, 4 g carbohydrates, 7 g total fat (3 g saturated fat), 50 mg cholesterol, 648 mg sodium

Hawaiian Shrimp Curry

You don't have to go to Hawaii to capture the flavor of the Islands—just reach for a can of coconut milk and some condiments.

⅓   **cup butter or margarine**

1   **tablespoon curry powder**

2   **teaspoons ground ginger**

½   **teaspoon pepper**

¼ cup finely minced onion

¼ cup water

7 tablespoons all-purpose flour

2 cups milk

1 cup unsweetened coconut milk
    or 2 cups cream or milk

1½ tablespoons lemon juice

1½ pounds medium-size cooked
    shrimp, shelled and deveined
    Salt
    Hot cooked rice
    Curry Condiments
    (suggestions follow)

Melt butter in a large pan over low
heat. Add curry powder, ginger, and
pepper; cook, stirring constantly,
until spices give off a nutty odor and
darken slightly in color (do not let
spices scorch).

Add onion and cook over medium
heat, stirring often, until golden (about
10 minutes). Add water and simmer,
uncovered, until liquid has evaporated and onion is very soft. Stir in
flour and cook, stirring, for 1 minute
(do not brown).

Remove pan from heat. Gradually
stir in milk and coconut milk. (If you
want a smooth sauce, pour mixture
into a blender at this point and whirl
until smooth.) Return pan to medium
heat and cook, stirring often, until
sauce boils and thickens.

Stir lemon juice and shrimp into
sauce; season to taste with salt. Heat,
stirring, just until shrimp are heated
through. Serve with rice; offer condiments to add to taste. Makes 4 to 6
servings.

Curry Condiments. Arrange in separate small bowls: chopped **peanuts,**
crumbled **crisp-cooked bacon, mango
chutney,** chopped **green bell pepper**
or onion (or a mixture of the two),
melon balls, papaya chunks, diced
banana (coated with **lemon juice**),
and **toasted flaked coconut.**

*Per serving: 396 calories (59 percent from fat), 24
g protein, 17 g carbohydrates, 26 g total fat (18 g
saturated fat), 222 mg cholesterol, 381 mg sodium*

Scampi

Also known as langostinos and
Dublin Bay prawns, *scampi* are small,
lobsterlike crustaceans fished from
the Adriatic Sea. Because true scampi
are hard to find in the United States,
we've substituted medium-size
shrimp. Simply sauté the shellfish in
butter with plenty of garlic and parsley.

¼ cup butter or margarine

1 tablespoon thinly sliced green
    onion

1 tablespoon olive oil or salad oil

4 or 5 cloves garlic, minced or
    pressed

2 teaspoons lemon juice

¼ teaspoon salt
    About ¾ pound medium-size
    raw shrimp, shelled (except for
    tails) and deveined

¼ teaspoon grated lemon peel

2 tablespoons minced parsley
    Dash of liquid hot pepper
    seasoning
    Lemon wedges

Melt butter in a wide frying pan over
medium heat. Stir in onion, oil, garlic,
lemon juice, and salt; cook, stirring
often, until bubbly. Add shrimp and
cook, stirring occasionally, until
opaque in center; cut to test (about 5
minutes). Stir in lemon peel, parsley,
and hot pepper seasoning. Serve with
lemon wedges. Makes 2 servings.

*Per serving: 423 calories (69 percent from fat), 29
g protein, 4 g carbohydrates, 32 g total fat (16 g
saturated fat), 273 mg cholesterol, 717 mg sodium*

Shrimp Fajitas

Low in fat and high in protein, these
simple-to-prepare fajitas provide a
nutritious meal in a single package.
To make the dish, you fill soft flour
tortillas with a sauté of tender marinated shrimp, green bell peppers, and
onions.

1 pound medium-size raw
    shrimp, shelled and deveined

1 cup lightly packed chopped
    cilantro

1 clove garlic, minced or pressed

⅓ cup lime juice

4 to 6 flour tortillas (*each* about
    8 inches in diameter)

1 tablespoon salad oil

2 large green bell peppers, seeded
    and thinly sliced

1 large onion, thinly sliced

½ cup plain nonfat yogurt or sour
    cream
    Purchased green tomatillo salsa

In a medium-size bowl, stir together
shrimp, cilantro, garlic, and lime juice.
Let stand at room temperature for
20 minutes.

Meanwhile, stack tortillas, wrap in
foil, and heat in a 350° oven until
warm and soft (about 15 minutes).

Heat oil in a wide nonstick frying
pan over medium-high heat. Add bell
peppers and onion; cook, stirring
occasionally, until vegetables are soft
(about 5 minutes). Lift out vegetables
with a slotted spoon and keep warm.
Add shrimp mixture to pan and cook
over high heat, stirring often, just until
shrimp are opaque in center; cut to
test (about 3 minutes). Return vegetables to pan; stir to mix with shrimp.

Spoon shrimp mixture into tortillas,
top with yogurt, and roll to enclose
filling. Offer salsa to add to individual
servings. Makes 4 to 6 servings.

*Per serving: 262 calories (23 percent from fat), 20
g protein, 30 g carbohydrates, 7g total fat (1 g
saturated fat), 112 mg cholesterol, 299 mg sodium*

Ginger Shrimp

Ginger, prized for its spicy perfume and pungent flavor, is a popular seasoning in Asian cooking. Here, just 2 teaspoons of the grated fresh root add a lively acccent to a simple stir-fry of shrimp and vegetables.

- ¼ **cup white wine vinegar**
- 2 **tablespoons soy sauce**
- 5 **teaspoons sugar**
- 1 **teaspoon cornstarch**
- 3 **tablespoons salad oil**
- 2 **cloves garlic, minced or pressed**
- 2 **teaspoons grated fresh ginger**
- 1 **pound medium-size raw shrimp, shelled and deveined**
- 2 **stalks celery, cut into ½-inch-thick slanting slices**
- 1 **can (about 8 oz.) bamboo shoots, drained**
- ¼ **cup thinly sliced green onions**
- 1 **green onion, thinly sliced**

In a small bowl, stir together vinegar, soy sauce, sugar, and cornstarch. Set aside.

Heat 2 tablespoons of the oil in a wok or wide frying pan over medium-high heat. When oil is hot, add garlic and ginger and stir once. Then add shrimp and cook, stirring, just until opaque in center; cut to test (about 3 minutes). Remove shrimp mixture from pan and set aside.

Heat remaining 1 tablespoon oil in pan. Add celery, bamboo shoots, and the ¼ cup onions; cook, stirring, for 1 minute. Return shrimp to pan. Stir vinegar mixture and add to pan; then cook, stirring, until sauce boils and thickens (about 1 minute). Transfer shrimp mixture to a serving dish and sprinkle evenly with sliced onion. Makes 4 servings.

Per serving: 232 calories (46 percent from fat), 20 g protein, 11 g carbohydrates, 12 g total fat (2 g saturated fat), 140 mg cholesterol, 672 mg sodium

Coquilles St. Jacques in Butter

This classic French dish is prepared in a number of ways; some versions include a white sauce, while others feature a cheese topping. Our favorite variation is simpler and more traditional, adorning the scallops with nothing more than butter and parsley.

- 1½ **pounds sea scallops**
- 1½ **cups dry white wine; or ¾ cup *each* dry white wine and water**
- ⅓ **cup butter or margarine, melted**
- 2 **tablespoons chopped parsley Paprika**

Rinse and drain scallops, place in a wide frying pan, and add wine. Bring to a boil over high heat. Then reduce heat, cover, and simmer until scallops are opaque in center; cut to test (8 to 10 minutes). With a slotted spoon, lift out scallops; drain on paper towels. Let cool slightly, then cut into thick slices.

Arrange scallops in 4 scallop shells or individual casseroles. Spoon a fourth of the butter over top of each filled shell. Sprinkle 1½ teaspoons parsley over each; then sprinkle with paprika. Bake in a 350° oven until heated through (about 5 minutes). Makes 4 servings.

Per serving: 305 calories (53 percent from fat), 29 g protein, 4 g carbohydrates, 16 g total fat (10 g saturated fat), 97 mg cholesterol, 431 mg sodium

Batter-fried Squid

Beer is the secret ingredient in this succulent batter-fried squid. It's traditional to serve the crisp, golden morsels with a squeeze of lemon and a sprinkling of malt vinegar and salt.

- 2 **pounds small whole squid, cleaned**
- 1 **cup all-purpose flour**
- ½ **teaspoon paprika**
- ¼ **teaspoon salt**
- ⅛ **teaspoon pepper**
- 1 **cup beer**
  Salad oil
  All-purpose flour
  Malt vinegar
  Salt
  Lemon wedges

Cut hoods of squid crosswise into ½-inch-thick rings. Rinse rings and tentacles; drain. In a medium-size bowl, mix the 1 cup flour, paprika, the ¼ teaspoon salt, and pepper. Add beer and stir until smooth.

In a deep pan, heat 1½ to 2 inches of oil to 400°F on a deep-frying thermometer. Dust squid with flour; shake off excess. Then dip squid, a few pieces at a time, into batter. Let excess batter drip off; then gently lower squid into oil (do not crowd pan). Cook, turning once, until golden (about 30 seconds). Lift out, drain on paper towels, and keep warm. Offer vinegar and salt to add to taste. Serve with lemon wedges. Makes 4 servings.

Per serving: 327 calories (28 percent from fat), 30 g protein, 25 g carbohydrates, 9 g total fat (2 g saturated fat), 413 mg cholesterol, 183 mg sodium

Two seafood stews—one from California, the other from Spain—provide a wonderful showcase for your favorite fish and shellfish.

San Francisco–style Cioppino

San Francisco is the birthplace of *cioppino*, but the exact origin of this Western classic is still unclear. Many attribute the dish to the Italian immigrants who worked on Meigg's Wharf, now known as Fisherman's Wharf, at the turn of the century.

Sunset has featured many variations of cioppino, each incorporating a different selection of Pacific seafood; this version uses shellfish alone.

¼ **cup olive oil or salad oil**

1 **large onion, sliced**

2 **large cloves garlic, minced or pressed**

1 **green bell pepper, seeded and diced**

⅓ **cup chopped parsley**

1 **large can (about 28 oz.) tomatoes**

1 **can (about 15 oz.) tomato sauce**

1 **cup dry red or white wine**

1 **dry bay leaf**

1 **teaspoon dry basil**

½ **teaspoon dry oregano**

12 **small hard-shell clams in shell, scrubbed**

1 **pound large raw shrimp, shelled and deveined**

2 **medium-size cooked Dungeness crabs (1½ to 2 lbs. *each*), cleaned and cracked**

Salt and pepper

Heat oil in a 6- to 8-quart pan over medium heat. Add onion, garlic, bell pepper, and parsley; cook, stirring often, until onion is soft (about 5 minutes). Chop tomatoes; add tomatoes and their liquid, tomato sauce, wine, bay leaf, basil, and oregano to pan. Bring to a boil; then reduce heat, cover, and simmer for 20 minutes.

Add clams, shrimp, and crabs. Cover and simmer until clams pop open and shrimp are opaque in center; cut to test (about 20 minutes). Discard unopened clams. Season to taste with salt and pepper. Makes 6 servings.

Per serving: 294 calories (35 percent from fat), 30 g protein, 18 g carbohydrates, 11 g total fat (2 g saturated fat), 141 mg cholesterol, 944 mg sodium

Spicy Seafood Paella

Spain's famous *paella* originated in the Atlantic port of Valencia—but today, each region along the coast has its own version of the hearty stew. The basics are agreed on: olive oil, saffron, and rice. Beyond that, the cook's imagination and the resources at hand determine the final recipe.

Paella takes its name from the traditional cooking utensil, a round, flat two-handled iron pan. If you don't have a paella pan, a heavy casserole dish or wide frying pan will do just as well.

¼ **cup olive oil**

1 **pound chorizo sausages, casings removed**

1 **green bell pepper, halved and seeded**

1 **medium-size red onion, chopped**

4 **large cloves garlic, minced or pressed**

½ **to 1 teaspoon crushed red pepper flakes**

2½ **cups long-grain rice**

3 **cups bottled clam juice**

½ **cup water**

1 **cup dry white wine**

¼ **teaspoon *each* saffron threads and black pepper**

1 **teaspoon salt**

½ **teaspoon dry basil**

1 **package (about 9 oz.) frozen artichoke hearts, thawed and drained**

1½ **pounds firm-textured white-fleshed fish fillets**

12 **small hard-shell clams in shell, scrubbed**

1 **pound medium-size raw shrimp, shelled and deveined**

12 **mussels in shell, scrubbed**

1 **pound cooked crab legs in shell, cracked**

1 **red bell pepper, seeded and cut into ¼-inch-wide strips**

Heat oil in a 14-inch paella pan or 4-quart ovenproof pan over medium-high heat. Crumble chorizo into pan and cook, stirring often, until lightly browned. Coarsely chop half the green bell pepper; cut remaining half into ¼-inch-wide strips and set aside. Add chopped bell pepper, onion, garlic, and red pepper flakes to pan; cook, stirring often, until onion is soft (about 5 minutes). Stir in rice, clam juice, water, wine, saffron, black pepper, salt, basil, and artichokes. Bring mixture to a boil over high heat. Then remove from heat, cover, and bake in a 350° oven for 30 minutes, stirring twice. Meanwhile, rinse fish, pat dry, and cut into 1-inch pieces.

Stir rice mixture. Then stir in fish. Push clams, shrimp, and mussels into rice. Arrange crab on top. Cover and continue to bake until rice is tender to bite, clams pop open, and shrimp are opaque in center; cut to test (about 15 more minutes). Discard any unopened clams. Garnish paella with green and red bell pepper strips and serve at once. Makes 6 to 8 servings.

Per serving: 857 calories (40 percent from fat), 60 g protein, 62 g carbohydrates, 37 g total fat (11 g saturated fat), 205 mg cholesterol, 818 mg sodium

*T*he Western cook has long enjoyed beef and chicken in a wide range of cuts. And at Sunset, we've come up with delicious recipes for all of them. Here we keep an eye towards varied cooking methods and international flavors. • Whether using tender or leaner cuts, versatile beef packs a lot of flavor. Paired with other distinctive flavors — bell peppers, corn, or peanuts—beef is still in favor. • Low in fat, low in cost, and easy to prepare, poultry ranks among favorite main dishes. Chicken offers a versatility and availability unparalleled by other meats. • With the current focus on light dining, modern poultry recipes are often designed to be lean. That doesn't mean that time-honored classics like chicken cacciatore, enchiladas, and pan-fried cutlets have been forgotten. On the contrary, they still top the list of Sunset's reader favorites!

Oven-simmered Beef Brisket

Oven-simmered in wine and soy, this succulent brisket is a comfort-food favorite. Serve it hot from the oven or refrigerate to slice for sandwiches.

2½ **cups sweet vermouth or apple juice**
½ **cup soy sauce**
¼ **cup salad oil**
2 **dry bay leaves**
1 **clove garlic, minced or pressed**
1 **large onion, chopped**
½ **teaspoon ground ginger**
¼ **teaspoon pepper**
1 **beef brisket (about 4 lbs.), trimmed of fat**
¼ **cup cornstarch blended with ¼ cup cold water (if serving meat hot)**

In a large baking pan, combine vermouth, soy sauce, oil, bay leaves, garlic, onion, ginger, and pepper; mix lightly. Add brisket; turn to coat. Cover and refrigerate, turning meat occasionally, until next day.

Leave meat in marinade and bake, covered, in a 350° oven until tender when pierced (about 3 hours). Transfer meat to a serving dish. Skim and discard fat from pan juices; discard bay leaves.

To serve brisket hot, stir cornstarch mixture into pan juices. Cook over medium heat, stirring constantly, until sauce is thickened; offer sauce to spoon over individual servings.

To serve brisket cold, omit cornstarch mixture. Return meat to pan juices and let cool; then cover and refrigerate until cold or for up to 2 days. Lift out meat and cut across the grain into thin slices. Makes 8 to 10 servings.

Per serving: 432 calories (45 percent from fat), 43 g protein, 15 g carbohydrates, 21 g total fat (6 g saturated fat), 125 mg cholesterol, 1,081 mg sodium

Spoonbread Tamale Pie

When *Sunset* printed this recipe in 1966, tamale pies were already long-time favorites with Western cooks.

Cornmeal Topping (recipe follows)
¼ **cup salad oil or olive oil**
1½ **pounds lean ground beef**
1 **large onion, chopped**
1 **small green bell pepper, seeded and chopped**
1 **clove garlic, minced or pressed**
1 **can (about 14½ oz.) tomatoes**
1 **can (about 12 oz.) whole-kernel corn**
1 **teaspoon salt**
4 **to 6 teaspoons chili powder**
¼ **teaspoon pepper**
½ **cup yellow cornmeal**
1 **cup water**
1 **cup pitted ripe olives**

Prepare Cornmeal Topping; set aside.

Heat oil in wide frying pan over medium heat. Crumble in beef; then add onion, bell pepper, and garlic. Cook, stirring often, until onion is golden (about 10 minutes). Cut up tomatoes; stir in tomatoes and their liquid, corn, salt, chili powder, and pepper. Bring to a boil; then reduce heat, cover, and simmer for 5 minutes.

In a small bowl, mix cornmeal and water; stir into meat. Simmer, uncovered, stirring occasionally, for 10 minutes. Stir in olives. Pour mixture into a 9- by 13-inch baking dish; spread with Cornmeal Topping. Bake in a 375° oven until topping is golden brown (about 40 minutes). Makes 8 servings.

Cornmeal Topping. In a small pan, combine 1½ cups **milk,** ½ teaspoon **salt,** and 2 tablespoons **butter** or margarine. Bring mixture to a simmer over medium-low heat. Gradually add ½ cup **yellow cornmeal;** cook, stirring,

until thickened. Remove from heat; stir in 1 cup (about 4 oz.) shredded **Cheddar cheese** and 2 **eggs,** beaten.

Per serving: 559 calories (60 percent from fat), 25 g protein, 31 g carbohydrates, 37 g total fat (14 g saturated fat), 146 mg cholesterol, 990 mg sodium

Flank Steak with Mustard-Caper Sauce

Dijon mustard and capers meet in a piquant sauce for rare flank steak.

¼ **cup butter or margarine**
1 **tablespoon olive oil or salad oil**
1 **flank steak (about 1½ lbs.), trimmed of fat**
3 **tablespoons dry vermouth or dry white wine**
1 **tablespoon Dijon mustard**
¼ **teaspoon Worcestershire**
1½ **tablespoons drained capers**

Melt 1 tablespoon of the butter in oil in a wide frying pan over medium-high heat. Add meat and cook, turning once, until well browned on both sides; cut to test (6 to 8 minutes for rare).

Transfer meat to a carving board and keep warm. Reduce heat under frying pan to low; add remaining 3 tablespoons butter, vermouth, mustard, Worcestershire, and capers. Stir to blend. Cut meat across the grain into thin slanting slices. Arrange in a serving dish or on individual plates and top with sauce. Makes 4 servings.

Per serving: 416 calories (63 percent from fat), 35 g protein, 2 g carbohydrates, 28 g total fat (13 g saturated fat), 116 mg cholesterol, 441 mg sodium

Enchilada Pie

We still receive frequent requests for this enchilada casserole, which was already a favorite back in 1955.

- **1 pound lean ground beef**
- **1 onion, chopped**
- **1 tablespoon chili powder**
- **1 can (about 8 oz.) tomato sauce**
  Salt and pepper
- **6 corn tortillas, spread with butter or margarine**
- **1 can (about 4 oz.) chopped ripe olives, drained**
- **1½ cups (about 6 oz.) shredded sharp Cheddar cheese**
- **½ cup water**

Crumble beef into a wide frying pan. Add onion and cook over medium heat, stirring often, until meat is browned. Stir in chili powder and tomato sauce. Season to taste with salt and pepper. In a 2-quart round baking dish, alternate layers of buttered tortillas, meat sauce, olives, and cheese. Pour water over top.

Cover and bake in a 400° oven until cheese is melted and tortilla stack is hot in center (about 20 minutes). Makes 4 to 6 servings.

Per serving: 541 calories (63 percent from fat), 28 g protein, 23 g carbohydrates, 38 g total fat (18 g saturated fat), 116 mg cholesterol, 857 mg sodium

Joe's Special

Joe's Special had already been a San Francisco favorite for over two generations when we printed this recipe in 1968. A hearty mixture of beef, onions, spinach, and eggs, it makes a satisfying meal at any time of day or night.

- **2 tablespoons olive oil or salad oil**
- **2 pounds lean ground beef**
- **2 medium-size onions, finely chopped**
- **2 cloves garlic, minced or pressed**
- **½ pound mushrooms, sliced (optional)**
- **1¼ teaspoons salt**
- **¼ teaspoon *each* ground nutmeg, pepper, and dry oregano**
- **1 package (about 10 oz.) frozen chopped spinach, thawed and squeezed dry; or ½ pound fresh spinach, rinsed, stems removed, and leaves chopped (about 4 cups)**
- **4 to 6 eggs, lightly beaten**

Heat oil in a wide frying pan over high heat. Crumble in beef and cook, stirring often, until browned. Add onions, garlic, and, if desired, mushrooms; reduce heat to medium and cook, stirring occasionally, until onions are soft (about 5 minutes). Stir in salt, nutmeg, pepper, oregano, and spinach; cook for about 5 more minutes. Add eggs. Reduce heat to low and cook, stirring constantly, just until eggs are softly set. Makes 6 servings.

Per serving: 537 calories (68 percent from fat), 34 g protein, 8 g carbohydrates, 40 g total fat (15 g saturated fat), 291 mg cholesterol, 651 mg sodium

Singapore Satay

A spicy, mildly sweet peanut sauce is the flavorful secret to successful satay. This version of the popular Asian dish can be made with your choice of meat or poultry. It's adapted from a recipe that won raves from *Sunset* editors during a culinary tour of Singapore in the early '70s.

- **3 to 4 pounds lean boneless meat, such as beef sirloin or top round, lamb shoulder or leg, or chicken breast or thigh (use one kind or a combination)**
- **2 tablespoons curry powder**
- **½ cup olive oil or salad oil**
- **½ cup soy sauce**
- **4 cloves garlic, minced or pressed**
- **2 tablespoons sugar**
  Peanut Sauce (recipe follows); or 2½ cups purchased peanut sauce

Cut meat into ¾-inch cubes, keeping different kinds of meat separate.

In a small bowl, stir together curry powder, oil, soy sauce, garlic, and sugar. Place meat cubes in a large bowl; pour marinade over meat cubes. (Or, if you use more than one kind of meat, put each in a heavy-duty plastic bag, set bags together in a bowl, and pour marinade into each one.) Cover (or seal bags) and refrigerate for at least 4 hours or up to 2 days; stir meat or turn bags over occasionally.

If using bamboo skewers, soak them in water to cover for 30 minutes. Prepare Peanut Sauce; keep warm.

Thread meat on long, sturdy bamboo or metal skewers (use only one kind of meat on each skewer). Place skewers on a grill about 2 inches above a solid bed of medium-hot coals. Cook, turning frequently, until meat is browned (8 to 10 minutes). Offer skewers of meat alongside dishes of Peanut Sauce for dipping. Makes 8 to 10 servings.

Peanut Sauce. In a blender or food processor, whirl 1 cup **salted peanuts** until finely ground; remove from blender and set aside.

Add 1 large **onion** (cut into 1-inch chunks), 2 cloves **garlic,** and 4 or 5 **small dried hot red chiles** to blender; whirl until smooth. Heat 2 tablespoons **salad oil** in a frying pan over medium heat. Add onion mixture, 2 teaspoons **ground coriander,** and 1 teaspoon **ground cumin;** cook, stirring occasionally, for 5 minutes.

Reduce heat to low and add ground peanuts. Then gradually stir in 1 can (about 12 oz.) **frozen unsweetened coconut milk** (thawed), 3 tablespoons firmly packed **brown sugar,** and 2 tablespoons *each* **lemon juice** and **soy sauce.** Bring sauce to a simmer; then continue to simmer (do not boil), uncovered, stirring occasionally, until sauce is thickened (about 15 minutes).

Serve sauce warm or at room temperature in wide, shallow rimmed dishes. If made ahead, let cool; then cover and refrigerate until next day. Reheat just until warm before serving. Makes about 2½ cups.

Per serving of meat: 325 calories (45 percent from fat), 41 g protein, 3 g carbohydrates, 16 g total fat (5 g saturated fat), 118 mg cholesterol, 545 mg sodium

Per tablespoon of Peanut Sauce: 52 calories (72 percent from fat), 1 g protein, 3 g carbohydrates, 4 g total fat (2 g saturated fat), 0 mg cholesterol, 83 mg sodium

Golden Chicken Cutlets

Triple-coated sautéed chicken breasts are juicy on the inside, delicately crunchy on the outside. A smooth reduction sauce, made from dry white wine and the pan juices, enhances the meat. Alongside, you might serve one of our vegetable recipes.

⅓ **cup all-purpose flour**
½ **teaspoon salt**
⅛ **teaspoon** *each* **white pepper, ground nutmeg, and dry marjoram**
1 **egg**
1 **tablespoon water**
⅓ **cup fine dry bread crumbs**
¼ **cup grated Parmesan cheese**
6 **skinless, boneless chicken breast halves (about 2¼ lbs. total)**

¼ **cup butter or margarine**
2 **tablespoons olive oil**
½ **cup dry white wine**
   Lemon wedges

Prepare 3 shallow dishes. In first dish, mix flour, salt, white pepper, nutmeg, and marjoram. In second dish, lightly beat egg with water. In third dish, mix crumbs and cheese. Set dishes aside.

Rinse chicken and pat dry. Place each breast half between 2 sheets of plastic wrap or wax paper; pound with a flat-surfaced mallet until about ¼ inch thick.

Working with one piece of chicken at a time, coat each piece lightly with flour mixture and shake off excess; then coat with egg and let excess drip off. Finally, coat with crumb mixture and shake off excess; secure remaining crumbs by pressing gently but firmly with your hand.

Melt butter in oil in a wide frying pan over medium-high heat. Add chicken, a few pieces at a time (do not crowd pan); cook, turning once, until golden brown on both sides (4 to 6 minutes). As chicken is cooked, transfer it to a serving dish and keep warm.

When all chicken has been cooked, add wine to frying pan and stir to scrape browned bits free. Bring sauce to a boil over high heat; boil, stirring, until sauce is slightly thickened. Pour sauce over chicken. Serve with lemon wedges. Makes 6 servings.

Per serving: 385 calories (41 percent from fat), 43 g protein, 10 g carbohydrates, 16 g total fat (7 g saturated fat), 157 mg cholesterol, 496 mg sodium

Slivered Chicken & Walnuts

Since stir-frying goes so quickly, assemble all of the ingredients before heating your wok or frying pan.

   Cooking Sauce (recipe follows)
1 **tablespoon soy sauce**
1 **teaspoon cornstarch**
1 **pound skinless, boneless chicken breasts, cut into thin strips**
3 **tablespoons salad oil**
½ **cup walnut halves**
1 **medium-size green bell pepper, seeded and cut into 1-inch squares**
½ **teaspoon finely minced fresh ginger or ⅛ teaspoon ground ginger**

Prepare Cooking Sauce; set aside. In a medium-size bowl, stir together soy sauce and cornstarch. Add chicken and stir to coat; set aside.

Place a wok or wide frying pan over medium-high heat. When pan is hot, add oil. When oil is hot, add walnuts and cook, stirring, until browned; remove from pan with a slotted spoon and set aside. Add chicken to pan; cook, stirring, for 1½ minutes. Remove from pan with slotted spoon. Add bell pepper and ginger; cook, stirring, until pepper turns bright green. Return chicken to pan. Stir Cooking Sauce, add to pan, and cook, stirring, until sauce boils and thickens (about 1 minute). Add walnuts, stir once, and serve. Makes 4 servings.

Cooking Sauce. In a small bowl, stir together ½ teaspoon **cornstarch,** a dash of **liquid hot pepper seasoning,** ¾ teaspoon *each* **sugar** and **wine vinegar,** 1 teaspoon **dry sherry** or water, and 1 tablespoon **soy sauce.**

Per serving: 330 calories (57 percent from fat), 29 g protein, 7 g carbohydrates, 21 g total fat (2 g saturated fat), 66 mg cholesterol, 592 mg sodium

Honeyed Chicken

Here's another delicious reader contribution from our "Kitchen Cabinet": chicken breasts basted with a sweet honey-mustard glaze. For a pretty presentation, accompany the chicken with Broccoli with Pine Nuts & Rice (page 32) or our Vegetable Risotto (page 43).

- 6 **skinless, boneless chicken breast halves (about 2¼ lbs. *total*)**
- 2 **tablespoons sesame seeds**
- 3 **tablespoons honey**
- ¼ **cup *each* dry sherry and Dijon mustard**
- 1 **tablespoon lemon juice**

Rinse chicken and pat dry. Then arrange pieces, slightly apart, in a 9- by 13-inch baking pan. Set aside.

Toast sesame seeds in a small frying pan over medium heat, stirring often, until golden (2 to 3 minutes). Transfer to a small bowl and add honey, sherry, mustard, and lemon juice; stir until blended. Drizzle honey mixture evenly over chicken. Bake in a 400° oven, basting several times with sauce, until meat in thickest part is no longer pink; cut to test (15 to 20 minutes). Makes 6 servings.

Per serving: 264 calories (16 percent from fat), 40 g protein, 12 g carbohydrates, 4 g total fat (0.8 g saturated fat), 99 mg cholesterol, 413 mg sodium

Cashew Chicken

Quick stir-frying intensifies the flavors of pea pods, tender mushrooms, green onions, and golden cashews in this colorful dish.

- 6 **skinless, boneless chicken breast halves (about 2¼ lbs. *total*)**
- ¼ **cup soy sauce**
- 2 **tablespoons cornstarch**
- ½ **teaspoon *each* sugar and salt**
- ¼ **cup salad oil**
- ⅓ **cup salted roasted cashews**
- ½ **pound Chinese pea pods (also called snow or sugar peas), ends and strings removed; or 2 packages (about 6 oz. *each*) frozen Chinese pea pods, partially thawed**
- ½ **pound mushrooms, sliced**
- 1 **tablespoon instant chicken bouillon dissolved in 1 cup hot water; or 1 cup chicken broth**
- 2 **cans (about 8 oz. *each*) bamboo shoots, drained and slivered**
- 4 **green onions, cut into thin slanting slices**

Rinse chicken and pat dry. Cut each piece crosswise into ⅛-inch-thick slices; then cut slices into 1-inch squares. Set aside. In a small bowl, stir together soy sauce, cornstarch, sugar, and salt; set aside.

Place a wok or wide frying pan over medium-high heat. When pan is hot, add 1 tablespoon of the oil. When oil is hot, add cashews and cook, stirring, until lightly browned; remove with a slotted spoon and set aside. Add remaining 3 tablespoons oil to pan. When oil is hot, add chicken and cook, stirring, until no longer pink. Add pea pods, mushrooms, and bouillon. Cover and simmer for 2 minutes.

Add bamboo shoots; then stir soy sauce mixture and add to pan. Cook, stirring, until sauce is thickened; then simmer, uncovered, for 1 minute. Add onions; stir until combined. Transfer to a large serving dish and sprinkle with cashews. Makes 6 to 8 servings.

Per serving: 316 calories (37 percent from fat), 38 g protein, 11 g carbohydrates, 13 g total fat (2 g saturated fat), 85 mg cholesterol, 1,298 mg sodium

Grilled Peanut Chicken

Smoldering wood chips impart a delicate smokiness to Asian-inspired chicken cooked on the grill.

- 2 **cups hickory or other wood chips**
- 4 **chicken breast halves (about 2 lbs. *total*)**
- ⅓ **cup *each* creamy peanut butter and warm water**
- 2 **tablespoons *each* soy sauce and Worcestershire**
- ¼ **to ½ teaspoon ground red pepper (cayenne)**
- 2 **tablespoons sliced green onion**
- ¼ **cup finely shredded fresh basil**

Soak wood chips in warm water to cover for at least 30 minutes or for up to 4 hours.

Rinse chicken and pat dry. In a large bowl, stir together peanut butter, the ⅓ cup warm water, soy sauce, Worcestershire, and red pepper until blended. Add chicken; turn to coat.

Drain wood chips and scatter over a solid bed of medium-low coals in a barbecue with a lid. Set grill 4 to 6 inches above coals; lightly grease grill. Lift chicken from sauce; place on grill.

Cover barbecue and close vents about three-fourths of the way. Cook chicken, turning and basting every 5 minutes with sauce, until meat in thickest part is no longer pink; cut to test (25 to 30 minutes).

To serve, arrange chicken in a serving dish and sprinkle with onion and basil. Makes 4 servings.

Per serving: 384 calories (48 percent from fat), 44 g protein, 7 g carbohydrates, 20 g total fat (4 g saturated fat), 103 mg cholesterol, 785 mg sodium

Chicken Cacciatore

In Italian-American culinary lingo, a *cacciatore* ("hunters'-style") dish is usually prepared like this—simmered with mushrooms, onions, bell pepper, white wine, and tomatoes.

- 4 **whole chicken legs (2 to 2½ lbs. *total*)**
- 2 **tablespoons butter or margarine**
- 1 **tablespoon olive oil**
- ½ **pound mushrooms, sliced**
- 1 **large onion, sliced**
- 2 **green bell peppers, seeded and finely chopped**
- 2 **cloves garlic, minced or pressed**
- ½ **cup dry white wine or chicken broth**
- 1 **can (about 15 oz.) tomato sauce**
- ¼ **teaspoon *each* dry marjoram, dry oregano, and dry thyme**
- 1 **teaspoon instant chicken bouillon**
- 2 **tablespoons minced parsley Salt**

Rinse chicken and pat dry.

Melt butter in oil in a wide frying pan over medium-high heat. Add chicken and cook, turning as needed, until browned on all sides. Remove from pan and set aside. Add mushrooms, onion, bell peppers, and garlic to pan and cook, stirring, until onion is soft (about 5 minutes). Stir in wine, tomato sauce, marjoram, oregano, thyme, bouillon, and parsley.

Return chicken to pan. Bring liquid to a boil over high heat. Then reduce heat, cover, and simmer until meat near thighbone is no longer pink; cut to test (about 30 minutes). If sauce is too thin, transfer chicken to a serving dish and keep warm. Bring sauce to a boil; boil, stirring, until slightly thickened. Season sauce to taste with salt; pour over chicken. Makes 4 servings.

Per serving: 512 calories (56 percent from fat), 38 g protein, 19 g carbohydrates, 32 g total fat (10 g saturated fat), 170 mg cholesterol, 1,096 mg sodium

Chutney-glazed Chicken Thighs

No fuss, no frills—just savory goodness. Serve this tangy-sweet glazed chicken with one of our readers' favorite side dishes. Try Wild Rice with Golden Raisins or Rice Pilaf with Fruit & Nuts (pages 42–43).

- **Vegetable oil cooking spray**
- 8 **chicken thighs (about 2 lbs. *total*)**
- ⅓ **cup Major Grey's or other chutney, chopped**

Spray a 12- by 15-inch baking pan with cooking spray. Rinse chicken and pat dry. Arrange chicken pieces, skin side up and slightly apart, in pan.

Bake in a 400° oven until meat near thighbone is no longer pink; cut to test (35 to 40 minutes). Brush chicken pieces evenly with chutney. Return to oven and bake just until glaze is set (about 5 more minutes). Makes 4 servings.

Per serving: 356 calories (48 percent from fat), 29 g protein, 16 g carbohydrates, 18 g total fat (5 g saturated fat), 109 mg cholesterol, 331 mg sodium

Chicken Yogurt Enchilada Bake

Yogurt stands in for the original sour cream in this updated 1950s-style layered casserole.

- ¼ **cup butter or margarine**
- ¼ **cup all-purpose flour**
- 2 **cups chicken broth**
- 1 **cup plain yogurt**
- 1 **large can (about 7 oz.) diced green chiles**
- 12 **corn tortillas**
- 2 **cups bite-size pieces of cooked chicken**
- 1 **small onion, chopped**
- 2 **cups (about 8 oz.) shredded jack cheese**
- ¼ **cup thinly sliced green onions**

Melt butter in a 1½- to 2-quart pan over medium heat. Add flour and cook, stirring, for 1 minute (do not brown). Gradually stir in broth; bring sauce to a boil, stirring constantly until smooth. Remove from heat and stir in yogurt and chiles. Spread a third of the sauce evenly over bottom of a 9- by 13-inch baking pan.

Quickly dip tortillas in water. Drain briefly and cut into 1-inch strips. Scatter half the tortilla strips over sauce, then cover evenly with chicken, chopped onion, two-thirds of the cheese, and half the remaining sauce. Top with remaining tortilla strips, remaining sauce, and remaining cheese. Cover and bake in a 400° oven until heated through (30 to 35 minutes); sprinkle with green onions. Makes 6 servings.

Per serving: 476 calories (48 percent from fat), 29 g protein, 34 g carbohydrates, 26 g total fat (7 g saturated fat), 100 mg cholesterol, 951 mg sodium

DESSERTS

Sweets are international favorites, whether they're served as dessert at the end of a meal or enjoyed with a cup of freshly brewed afternoon coffee or tea. Westerners often favor traditional down-home specialties like giant oatmeal chocolate chip cookies and tiny bite-sized brownies—they all are included in this chapter. ● But that doesn't mean we've overlooked recipes that have achieved their "best-loved" status more recently. Today's interest in Italian cooking has increased the popularity of biscotti—ours are lemon- and pistachio-flavored. In these pages, you'll also find an unusual macadamia nut torte that calls to mind the Hawiian Islands. And for a new flavor "twist" on an old-fashioned favorite, try spicy pumpkin and ice cream roll. ● Lower-fat desserts have also found a place here. Try our No-fat Chocolate Cake if your sweet tooth doesn't stop when the diet begins.

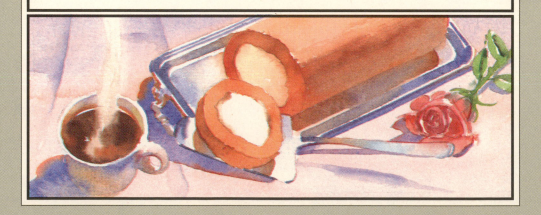

Big Oatmeal Chocolate Chip Cookies

Nearly 6 inches across and chewy with oatmeal, these oversized cookies always bring in the dough at bake sales. For variety, you can use butterscotch chips instead of chocolate ones.

- 1½ **cups all-purpose flour**
- 2 **teaspoons baking soda**
- 1 **teaspoon salt**
- 1 **cup (½ lb.) butter or margarine, at room temperature**
- 1½ **cups firmly packed brown sugar**
- 2 **eggs**
- 1 **teaspoon vanilla**
- 2⅓ **cups quick-cooking rolled oats**
- 1 **large package (about 12 oz.) semisweet chocolate or butterscotch-flavored chips**
- 1½ **cups chopped nuts**
  Granulated sugar

In a small bowl, mix flour, baking soda, and salt; set aside. In a large bowl, beat butter and brown sugar with an electric mixer or a heavy spoon until creamy. Beat in eggs and vanilla. Gradually add flour mixture, beating until well blended. Stir in oats, chocolate chips, and nuts.

Spoon ½-cup portions of dough onto greased baking sheets, spacing cookies 6 inches apart and 2½ inches from edges of sheets. Grease bottom of a pie pan, dip in granulated sugar, and use to flatten each cookie into a 5½-inch circle. If necessary, press cookies lightly with your fingers to give them an even thickness.

Bake cookies in a 350° oven until edges are lightly browned (about 15 minutes). Let cool on baking sheets for about 5 minutes; then transfer to racks to cool completely. Store airtight. Makes about 1 dozen cookies.

Per cookie: 627 calories (50 percent from fat), 9 g protein, 74 g carbohydrates, 36 g total fat (16 g saturated fat), 77 mg cholesterol, 574 mg sodium

No-fat Chocolate Cake

This mouthwatering cake's rich flavor is deceptive—the dessert is made entirely without fat.

- **Vegetable oil cooking spray**
  Cake flour
- 1 **cup sifted cake flour**
- ⅓ **cup unsweetened cocoa**
- 1 **teaspoon *each* baking soda and baking powder**
- 6 **egg whites**
- 1⅓ **cups firmly packed brown sugar**
- 1 **cup plain nonfat yogurt**
- 1 **teaspoon vanilla**
  Powdered sugar

Spray an 8-inch-square baking pan with cooking spray, dust with flour, and set aside. In a small bowl, mix the 1 cup flour, cocoa, baking soda, and baking powder; set aside. In a large bowl, beat egg whites, brown sugar, yogurt, and vanilla until blended. Add flour mixture; beat until evenly moistened. Pour batter into baking pan.

Bake in a 350° oven until center of cake springs back when lightly touched (30 to 40 minutes). Let cake cool in pan on a rack for 15 minutes; then turn out onto a serving plate. Sift powdered sugar over cake. Serve warm or cool. If made ahead, let cool; then cover and refrigerate for up to 2 days. Makes 8 servings.

Per serving: 222 calories (4 percent from fat), 6 g protein, 49 g carbohydrates, 1 g total fat (0.4 g saturated fat), 0.6 mg cholesterol, 293 mg sodium

PILGRIM JOE'S
Spiced Pumpkin Roll

Pumpkin desserts are traditional for Thanksgiving. If you're looking for a new one, try this pretty treat.

- ¾ **cup all-purpose flour**
- 2 **teaspoons ground cinnamon**
- 1 **teaspoon *each* baking powder and ground ginger**
- ½ **teaspoon *each* salt and ground nutmeg**
- 3 **eggs**
- 1 **cup granulated sugar**
- ⅔ **cup canned pumpkin**
  Powdered sugar
- 1 **quart toasted almond or vanilla ice cream, slightly softened**

Line bottom of a greased 10- by 15-inch rimmed baking pan with wax paper; grease paper.

In a small bowl, mix flour, cinnamon, baking powder, ginger, salt, and nutmeg; set aside. In a large bowl, beat eggs with an electric mixer on high speed until thick and lemon-colored. Gradually beat in granulated sugar. On low speed, beat in pumpkin, then flour mixture, until well blended. Spread batter evenly in pan. Bake in a 375° oven until center of cake springs back when lightly touched (about 15 minutes).

When cake is done, immediately turn it out of pan onto a towel sprinkled with powdered sugar. Peel off wax paper. Beginning at a long side, roll up cake and towel jelly-roll style; let cool completely. Unroll cake and remove towel; spread cake with ice cream and reroll to enclose ice cream. Wrap airtight and freeze until firm. Before serving, let stand at room temperature for 10 to 15 minutes; dust with powdered sugar. Cut crosswise into slices. Makes 8 to 10 servings.

Per serving: 288 calories (27 percent from fat), 5 g protein, 48 g carbohydrates, 9 g total fat (5 g saturated fat), 97 mg cholesterol, 250 mg sodium

Lemon-tipped Pistachio Biscotti

Dotted with pale green pistachios and tipped with a tangy lemon glaze, these twice-baked Italian cookies are surprisingly low in fat. Serve them with frothy espresso or alongside a fresh fruit sorbet for a light conclusion to a special meal.

- 2 **cups all-purpose flour**
- 2 **teaspoons baking powder**
- ¼ **cup butter or margarine, at room temperature**
- ⅔ **cup sugar**
- 1½ **teaspoons grated lemon peel**
- 1 **egg**
- 2 **egg whites**
- 1 **teaspoon vanilla**
- ½ **cup shelled salted roasted pistachio nuts, coarsely chopped**
  Lemon Icing (recipe follows)

In a medium-size bowl, mix flour and baking powder; set aside. In a large bowl, beat butter, sugar, and lemon peel until well blended. Beat in egg, then egg whites. Beat in vanilla. Gradually add flour mixture, beating until well blended. Stir in pistachios.

Divide dough in half. On a lightly floured board, shape each half into a long loaf about 1½ inches in diameter. Place loaves about 3 inches apart on a greased baking sheet; flatten each loaf to a thickness of about ½ inch. Bake in a 350° oven until firm to the touch (15 to 18 minutes).

Remove baking sheet from oven; cut hot loaves crosswise into about ½-inch-thick slices. Turn slices cut sides down and spread out slightly on baking sheets (you will need at least 2 baking sheets). Return to oven and continue to bake until cookies look dry and are lightly browned (about 10 more minutes). Transfer cookies to racks and let cool completely.

Prepare Lemon Icing; spread icing over about 1 inch of one end of each cookie. Let stand until icing is firm (about 15 minutes). Store airtight. Makes about 4½ dozen cookies.

Lemon Icing. In a small bowl, stir together 1 cup sifted **powdered sugar** and ½ teaspoon **grated lemon peel.** Stir in 1 to 1½ tablespoons **lemon juice,** using just enough to give icing a good spreading consistency.

Per cookie: 50 calories (28 percent from fat), 1 g protein, 8 g carbohydrates, 2 g total fat (0.6 g saturated fat), 6 mg cholesterol, 35 mg sodium

Kona Torte

Macadamias are undeniably expensive—but macadamia fans agree that the nut's rich flavor is well worth the price! Here, a buttery pastry shell holds a luscious filling of whole macadamias in caramel.

- 2½ **cups (about ¾ lb.) salted roasted macadamia nuts**
- 2¾ **cups all-purpose flour**
- 2½ **cups sugar**
- 1 **cup (½ lb.) butter or margarine, cut into chunks**
- 1 **egg**
- 1 **cup whipping cream**
- 1 **egg white, lightly beaten**
  Salted roasted macadamia nuts
  Sweetened whipped cream

Rub the 2½ cups macadamia nuts in a towel to remove salt; lift nuts from towel and set aside.

In a food processor (or a medium-size bowl), combine flour and ½ cup of the sugar. Add butter; whirl (or rub with your fingers) until mixture resembles fine crumbs. Add egg and whirl (or stir with a fork) until pastry holds together. Shape pastry into a ball.

Press two-thirds of the pastry evenly over bottom and up sides of a 9-inch spring-form pan. Cover and refrigerate. Place remaining pastry between 2 sheets of wax paper and roll out to a 9-inch round. Refrigerate flat until firm.

In a wide nonstick frying pan, heat remaining 2 cups sugar over medium-high heat, tilting and shaking pan often, until sugar melts and turns a pale amber color (about 6 minutes); watch closely, since sugar scorches easily. Pour in cream; caramelized sugar will harden. Cook, stirring, until mixture is melted and smooth. Remove from heat; stir in the 2½ cups nuts. Let cool for 10 to 20 minutes, then spoon into pastry shell.

Peel off one sheet of the wax paper from the pastry round and invert pastry over the nut filling. Peel off the remaining paper. If necessary, fold edge of pastry under to make flush with pan rim; press with tines of a flour-dipped fork to seal. Brush pastry with egg white.

Bake in a 325° oven until golden brown (about 1 hour). Let cool on a rack for 10 to 20 minutes. Run a sharp knife between torte and pan rim to loosen torte; remove pan rim and let torte cool completely. If made ahead, store airtight at room temperature for up to 2 days. To serve, garnish with macadamia nuts; then cut into thin wedges. Offer whipped cream to spoon over individual servings. Makes 14 to 16 servings.

Per serving: 532 calories (57 percent from fat), 5 g protein, 54 g carbohydrates, 34 g total fat (13 g saturated fat), 65 mg cholesterol, 237 mg sodium

Brownie Bites

Each of these miniature brownies can be eaten in a single luscious bite.

½ cup (¼ lb.) butter or margarine
4 ounces unsweetened chocolate
1½ cups sugar
1 teaspoon vanilla
3 eggs
1 cup all-purpose flour
About 40 walnut halves

Place butter and chocolate in a medium-size pan. Heat over low heat, stirring occasionally, until melted and smooth. Remove pan from heat and stir in sugar and vanilla. Add eggs, one at a time, beating well after each addition. Stir in flour.

Spoon batter into paper-lined tiny (1½-inch) muffin cups, filling cups almost to the top. Place a walnut half on top of batter in each cup. Bake in a 325° oven until tops of brownies look dry and feel firm when lightly touched (about 20 minutes). Let brownies cool in pans for 10 minutes; then transfer to racks to cool completely. Serve warm or cool. Store airtight. Makes about 40 cookies.

Per cookie: 94 calories (50 percent from fat), 1 g protein, 11 g carbohydrates, 6 g total fat (3 g saturated fat), 22 mg cholesterol, 29 mg sodium

Peach-Blueberry Crackle Brûlée

At *Sunset*, we've created numerous variations of crème brûlée. This impressive version combines smooth vanilla custard, fresh ripe fruit, and a lacy, golden caramel topping.

5 eggs
1¼ cups sugar
1¼ cups milk
1¼ cups whipping cream or half-and-half

1 teaspoon grated lemon peel
1½ teaspoons vanilla
½ teaspoon almond extract
¼ cup orange-flavored liqueur
2 medium-size firm-ripe peaches
1 tablespoon lemon juice
¼ cup fresh blueberries; or ¼ cup frozen unsweetened blueberries, thawed and drained

In a medium-size bowl, beat eggs and ¾ cup of the sugar until blended but not frothy. Stir in milk, cream, lemon peel, vanilla, almond extract, and liqueur.

Place a shallow 10-inch-round 1½-quart baking dish, such as a quiche or pie dish, in a larger pan (such as a roasting pan). Pour egg mixture into dish; pour boiling water into larger pan to a depth of about ½ inch.

Bake on middle of rack of a 350° oven until custard jiggles only slightly in center when dish is gently shaken (about 18 minutes). Lift custard from hot water and let cool on a rack; then cover and refrigerate for at least 1 hour or until next day.

Peel and halve peaches; cut each half into 4 wedges. Discard pits. In a small bowl, combine peaches and lemon juice; turn to coat peaches. Drain off lemon juice, then arrange peaches on custard, leaving a 1-inch border of custard. Scatter blueberries over peaches.

About 15 minutes before serving, place remaining ½ cup sugar in a medium-size nonstick frying pan. Over medium-high heat, tilt and shake pan often, until sugar melts and turns pale amber (about 8 minutes); watch closely—sugar scorches easily. Immediately remove from heat.

Tilt pan to pool caramel syrup on one side. Stir slowly with a long-handled metal teaspoon until syrup is thickened (1½ to 2 minutes).

Working quickly, pour syrup from spoon in a thin stream, crisscrossing

fruit and custard to create a lacy topping; use all the syrup. Let stand for about 3 minutes to let caramel syrup harden.

To serve, break through caramel topping with a spoon; then spoon out fruit and custard onto dessert plates. Makes 6 to 8 servings.

Per serving: 389 calories (43 percent from fat), 7 g protein, 47 g carbohydrates, 18 g total fat (10 g saturated fat), 205 mg cholesterol, 82 mg sodium

CHOCOLATE

The Aztecs discovered chocolate, which they called *xocolatl* (bitter water). Chocolate without sugar is indeed bitter; varying amounts of added sugar, milk solids, lecithin, and vanilla determine the variety of the finished chocolate. *Unsweetened* chocolate (chocolate liquor) is about 50% cocoa butter and contains no sugar or added ingredients; *bittersweet* chocolate contains at least 35% chocolate liquor; *sweet* chocolates can contain from 15–35%; *milk* chocolate must contain at least 12% milk solids and 10% chocolate liquor. *White* chocolate is not chocolate at all: it contains no chocolate liquor but it does contain cocoa butter.

INDEX